STATE V. BURNS

Sixth Edition

STATE V. BURNS

Sixth Edition

Donald H. Beskind

Professor of the Practice of Law
Duke University School of Law

Anthony J. Bocchino

Professor of Law
Temple University
Beasley School of Law
Philadelphia, Pennsylvania

NATIONAL INSTITUTE FOR TRIAL ADVOCACY

Address inquiries to:

Reprint Permission
National Institute for Trial Advocacy
1685 38th Street, Suite 200
Boulder, CO 80301-2735
Phone: (800) 225-6482
Fax: (720) 890-7069
E-mail: permissions@nita.org

ISBN 978-1-60156-397-2
FBA 1397

17 16 15 14   10 9 8 7 6 5 4 3 2 1
Printed in the United States of America

 Wolters Kluwer

Official co-publisher of NITA.
WKLegaledu.com/NITA

CONTENTS

INTRODUCTION

The Darrow County Grand Jury has charged John Burns with first-degree murder and robbery for the death of Rachel Carter Aboud and the armed robbery of the Aboud grocery store on May 9, YR-0, in Nita City, Nita.

Lauren Jones was attempting to rob the Aboud grocery store when the owner, Ali Aboud, pulled a gun from under the counter and fired at Mr. Jones. The bullet missed Jones and struck and killed Aboud's wife, Rachel. Jones was arrested at the scene of the robbery and has pleaded guilty to robbery. No murder charges are pending against him.

The State alleges that the defendant, John Burns, planned the robbery of the grocery store and waited outside in the getaway car while Jones went inside to rob the store. The defendant has been charged with armed robbery for his alleged participation in the holdup and with murder for the death of Mrs. Aboud.

The applicable law is contained in the statutes, case law, and proposed jury instructions that appear at the end of the case file.

All years in these materials are stated in the following form:

- YR-0 indicates the actual year in which the case is being tried (i.e., the present year);
- YR-1 indicates the next preceding year (please use the actual year);
- YR-2 indicates the second preceding year (please use the actual year), etc.

Authors' Note: The crime charged occurred in May, YR-0 [current year], and if the case file is used before June 1 in any given year, please backdate the dating system for all dates by one year. For example, YR-0 becomes YR-1; YR-1 becomes YR-2; YR-2 becomes the YR-3; etc.

SPECIAL INSTRUCTIONS FOR USE AS A FULL TRIAL

When this case file is used as the basis for a full trial, the following witnesses may be called by the parties:

For the State:
    Juan Perez – *officer*
    Ali Aboud – *store owner*
    Lauren Jones – *actual robber*

For the Defendant:
    John Burns – *D*
    Mary Burns – *D's wife* ⎤ *alibi*
    Laurence Roberts – *friend* ⎦ *witnesses*

A party need not call all of the persons listed as its witnesses. Any or all of the witnesses can be called by either party with the exceptions that the State cannot call the defendant and no party may call more than three witnesses. However, if a witness is to be called by a party other than the one for whom he or she is listed above, the party for whom the witness is listed will select and prepare the witness.

The defense made a pretrial motion to preclude any in-court identification of the defendant by Lauren Jones based on the suggestiveness of the show-up on May 12, Y-0. The motion was denied. Under Nita law, the ruling is appealable only if the defendant is convicted and chooses to raise the issue on appeal.

To do: (DIRECT = PEREZ & CROSS = BURNS)

* Perez introduce phone call @ 10:31am on Jones's phone
    — same day as gun reported stolen & crime committed
* Burns residence to Aboud's = 5-11 minutes depending on drive time

* Elements of armed robbery/first degree murder need to be proved —
    especially in closing. → Burns was indicted
            → pg. 97-99 has statutes & case law

* Perez issued a valid arrest warrant

* Perez saw Aboud in disturbed state

* Burns claims stolen weapon — what other evidence?

* Perez drew map of grocery — introduce & have him
    testify as to layout

* When Burns weapon was reported stolen = PEREZ

* Jones & Aboud = same description of vehicle

* If calling Aboud = ask if knows Jones
            → they both saw same type of car????

* Jones knew his testimony needed to be truthful in order
    to get ANY deal

* If Perez = bring up Jones plea deal → want that condition
    of deal was truthful info!!!

* Jones identified Burns in courtroom while 2 plain clothed
    officers were also present — Burns was in the middle

STIPULATIONS

The parties have agreed to the following stipulations:

1. All of the documents (including printouts) and newspaper clippings in the case file are authentic.

2. The Smith and Wesson .38 referred to in the case file is authentic.

3. The defendant has waived any right to a speedy trial.

4. May 9, YR-0, when the robbery occurred and Mrs. Aboud was killed, was a Saturday.

5. May 10, YR-0, was a Sunday, and it was Mother's Day.

6. The Nita Motor Vehicle Code requires that automobiles display front and rear license plates.

7. The log on Lauren Jones' cellphone showed a call from an unknown caller to his telephone at 10:31 a.m. on May 9, YR-0; Detective Perez may testify to this fact without the introduction of the actual cellphone.

8. A photo (to be provided by the prosecution) of Rachel Aboud is admissible.

9. As of the date of the trial, Patsy Burns has not had her surgery.

10. The driving time from the Burns residence to the Aboud store is five to eleven minutes, depending on the traffic.

IN THE SUPERIOR COURT OF DARROW COUNTY

STATE OF NITA

THE PEOPLE OF THE STATE OF NITA	)	Case No. YR-0 CR 324
	)	
vs.	)	
	)	INDICTMENT
JOHN BURNS	)	
	)	
Defendant.	)	

COUNT I—ARMED ROBBERY

The jurors of the Grand Jury of the State of Nita, within and for the county aforesaid, on their oaths, in the name and by the authority of the State of Nita, do find and present that John Burns, on the 9th day of YR-0, at the county aforesaid, did commit the crime of Armed Robbery in violation of Section 18-6-302 of the Nita Criminal Code of 2004, as amended, in that he, together with another, took a thing of value, United States currency, from the person and presence of Ali Aboud by the use of threats, force, and intimidation by displaying a deadly weapon, a gun, contrary to the form of the statute in such case made and provided, and against the peace and dignity of the State of Nita.

COUNT II—FIRST DEGREE MURDER

The jurors of the Grand Jury of the State of Nita, within and for the county aforesaid, on their oaths, in the name and by the authority of the State of Nita, further do find and present that John Burns, in violation of Section 18-6-102(1)(b) on the 9th day of YR-0, at the county aforesaid, committed an armed robbery, and in the course of and in furtherance of committing that crime, his co-participant, Lauren Jones, committed acts provocative of lethal resistance causing Ali Aboud to fire his .22 caliber gun, which killed Rachel Carter Aboud, contrary to the form of the statute in such case made and provided, and against the peace and dignity of the State of Nita.

In this true bill we are unanimous in our agreement.

This the 20th day of May, YR-0.

A TRUE BILL:

Ann Marie Alifano
Ann Marie Alifano
District Attorney

Bernadette Brown
Foreperson of the Grand Jury

STATE OF NITA

County of Darrow

In The General Court of Justice

Superior Court Division

The People of the State of Nita

File # YR-0 CR 324

vs.

John Burns, Defendant.

Address: 221 Elm St., Nita City, Nita

To any officer with authority and territorial jurisdiction to execute a warrant for arrest for the offense charged below:

THE UNDERSIGNED FINDS THAT THERE IS PROBABLE CAUSE TO BELIEVE that on or about the 9th day of May, YR-0, in the county named above, in violation of G.S.18-6-102(1)(b) and 18-6-302, the defendant named above, acting with Lauren Jones, committed an armed robbery of Aboud's IGA Market at 401 Main St., Nita City, Nita, and in the course of that armed robbery, Rachel Carter Aboud was killed when Lauren Jones committed an act provocative of lethal resistance, thereby proximately causing Ali Aboud to fire his .22 caliber gun thereby killing Rachel Carter Aboud.

YOU ARE DIRECTED TO ARREST THE DEFENDANT NAMED ABOVE AND BRING HIM WITHOUT UNNECESSARY DELAY BEFORE A JUDICIAL OFFICIAL TO ANSWER THE CHARGES SET OUT ABOVE.

Issued this 11th day of May, YR-0, upon information furnished under oath by the complainant or complainants named below

Complainant(s):
Ali Aboud
Juan Perez

Anne Beckman

Superior Court Judge

NITA CITY POLICE DEPARTMENT
NITA CITY, NITA

Lauren Jones

ARREST REPORT

1 ARREST NUMBER	2 PRINTS [X]	PHOTOS [X]	3 NAME LAST	FIRST	MIDDLE
3182-YR-0			Jones	Lauren	NMI

4 ALIAS/NICKNAME	5 DATE OF BIRTH	6 AGE	7 SEX	8 RACE/ETHNIC
Spike	7/31/YR-28	28	M	C

9 ADDRESS	PHONE	10 PLACE OF BIRTH
3300 Hillgrand Drive, Nita City, Nita	unknown	Meriden, Nita

11 HEIGHT	12 WEIGHT	13 HAIR	14 EYES	15 COMPLEXION	16 SOC. SEC. NUMBER
5'10"	160	Brown	Brown	Fair/clear	049-36-4748

17 OPERATOR LICENSE NUMBER & STATE	18 MISCELLANEOUS	19 OCCUPATION
N-5182564		Unemployed

20 EMPLOYEE/SCHOOL	21 ADDRESS	PHONE
N/A	N/A	unknown

DETAILS OF ARREST

22 DATE OF ARREST MO DAY YR	23 TIME 24 hr clock	24 HOW ARRESTED ON VIEW [X]	WARRANT [ ]	ORDER FOR ARREST [ ]
5/9/YR-0	1620			

25 PLACE OF ARREST
401 Main Street, Nita City, Nita (Aboud's IGA)

26 INITIAL CHARGE	27 COUNTS	28 STATUTE	29 OFFENSE JURISDICTION	30 WARRANT DATE MO DAY YR
Murder	1	18-6-102 (1)(b)	Nita City & Darrow County	N/A

31 SUBSEQUENT CHARGE	32 COUNTS	33 STATUTE	34 OFFENSE JURISDICTION	35 WARRANT DATE MO DAY YR
Armed robbery	1	18-6-302	Nita City & Darrow County	N/A

36 VEHICLE INFORMATION				37 PLACE STORED
LICENSE # N/A	STATE N/A	MAKE N/A	VIN N/A	N/A

38 VEHICLE INVENTORY INFORMATION MO DAY YR

39 COMPLAINANT'S NAME	ADDRESS	PHONE
Ali Aboud	61 Hill Avenue, Nita City, Nita	unknown

CONFINEMENT/BOND INFORMATION

40 DATE CONFINED MO DAY YR	TIME 24 Hour Clock	41 PLACE CONFINED	42 COMMITTING MAGISTRATE
5/9/YR-0	1650	Nita City Jail	Gregory S. Lewis

43 TYPE BOND	44 AMOUNT	45 DATE RELEASED MO DAY YR	TIME 24 HOUR CLOCK	46 RELEASED BY
None	N/A			N/A

DISPOSITION INFORMATION

47 DEPOSITION DATE MO DAY YR	48 COURT DOCKET	49 COURT/JUDGE	CITY
5/18/YR-0	YR-0-6969	Darrow County-Superior Court, Nita City	

50 DISPOSITION	51 SENTENCE
Plea. guilty robbery/murder dismissed with leave	Continued at request of District Attorney

day of crime   *Saturday*

52 NARRATIVE On 5/9/YR-0 I was summoned to Aboud's IGA Market at 401 Main St., Nita City, Nita, where there had been a reported armed robbery and shooting. I received the call at approximately 4:15 p.m. and proceeded directly to the scene of the offense. Upon arrival, I found the owner of the market, Ali Aboud, who was holding at gun point

RIGHT THUMB

53 ARRESTING OFFICER – NAME AND SIGNATURE	54 DATE/SUBMITTED MO DAY YR	TIME 24 Hour Clock
Detective Juan Perez, NCPD	5/12/YR-0	300

55 SUPERVISOR SIGNATURE	56 ARRESTEE SIGNATURE
J. McCormick	

NITA CITY POLICE DEPARTMENT
NITA CITY, NITA

ARREST REPORT—CONTINUATION PAGE

1 ARREST NUMBER	2 NAME LAST	FIRST	MIDDLE	3 ALIAS/NICKNAME
3182-YR-0	Jones	Lauren	NMI	Spike

4 COMPLAINANT'S NAME	ADDRESS	PHONE
Ali Aboud	61 Hill Avenue, Nita City, Nita	unknown

5 NARRATIVE

the defendant, Lauren Jones. I also discovered the owner's wife, Rachel Carter Aboud, lying in a pool of blood adjacent to the magazine rack along the front window of the store. Mrs. Aboud was apparently dead. An ambulance had already been summoned. I placed the defendant, Lauren Jones, under arrest for robbery and murder and obtained a statement from the owner, Mr. Aboud. He was in a very disturbed state, but I was able to ascertain the following facts. On 5/9/YR-0, the defendant, Lauren Jones, entered the above described premises at approximately 4:00 p.m. His face was covered with a blue and white bandana. He was pointing a pistol at Mr. Aboud and demanded all the money from the register while threatening Mr. Aboud by repeatedly, forcefully, and in an apparent state of agitation that he (Jones) would shoot Mr. Aboud and everyone else in the store if Mr. Aboud did not turn over the money. Jones got impatient and pushed the cash button on the register and grabbed some bills from the cash drawer. At that point, Mr. Aboud reached under the counter for his .22 pistol to shoot Jones. When the gun came out, Jones dropped the bills and dropped to floor as Mr. Aboud was firing his one shot. That shot missed Jones and hit Mrs. Aboud. Jones yelled out that his weapon was not loaded and not to shoot. Mr. Aboud, kept a gun trained on Jones and went to where his wife had fallen and talked to her briefly before she died. I was unable to ascertain the contents of their conversation before Mr. Aboud broke down completely. Defendant Jones was taken to police headquarters by Ofc. Yank of NCPD. I took into custody both the Aboud .22 and the defendant's weapon, a .38 Smith & Wesson pistol. I ascertained that the firing pin had been removed. Both weapons were placed in evidence bags, which I kept in my possession until I returned to the station house whereupon they were inventoried and secured in the evidence locker. Serial nos. on the two weapons are as follows: .22 caliber pistol 348X75H498; .38 caliber Smith & Wesson pistol V672952. I then drove Mr. Aboud to the home of his neighbor, Walter Dolan. At that point, Mr. Aboud had calmed down some and he could give me a more compete statement concerning the events in question. He gave me a signed statement that I typed up on my field computer and printed out on Mr. Dolan's printer that was witnessed by Mr. Dolan and myself. Later at the police station, I informed Mr. Jones again of his Miranda rights. I asked him if he understood his rights, and he responded in the affirmative. I then talked to him, and he gave a statement to the police stenographer, which he later signed with a notary present.

5/10/YR-0 Continued investigation in the above matter. Signed out .38 Smith & Wesson pistol from the evidence locker for the purpose of performing fingerprint analysis. Analysis indicated several prints matching those obtained from Lauren Jones were present on the gun butt and trigger. There was also one unidentified latent thumb print on top of the gun barrel just forward of the firing mechanism. The print was positioned so that the fingernail would have been pointing away from the end of the barrel towards the hammer and the rest of the finger towards the muzzle. Returned above-described pistol to the evidence locker and signed it back in. I once again spoke to the defendant Jones with his consent and he informed me that he had nothing further to say in the matter.

6 OFFICER'S NAME	7 OFFICER'S SIGNATURE
Detective Juan Perez	Juan Perez

8 DATE/SUBMITTED MO DAY YR TIME 24 Hour Clock	9 SUPERVISOR'S NAME	10
5/13/YR-0	J. McCormick	Page 2 of 4

[handwritten margin notes: "Facts from Ali Aboud", "— can testify to statement?", "— later Burns's print", "Sunday day after"]

NITA CITY POLICE DEPARTMENT
NITA CITY, NITA

ARREST REPORT—CONTINUATION PAGE

1 ARREST NUMBER	2 NAME LAST	FIRST	MIDDLE	3 ALIAS/NICKNAME
3182-YR-0	Jones	Lauren	NMI	Spike

4 COMPLAINANT'S NAME	ADDRESS	PHONE
Ali Aboud	61 Hill Avenue, Nita City, Nita	unknown

5 NARRATIVE

[handwritten left margin: Monday 2 days after]

5/11/YR-0 : Continued investigation in above matter. Jones was arraigned at 9:00 a.m. on first-degree murder and armed robbery charges. With Mr. Aboud's permission, I gained entrance into the premises at 401 Main Street and took various measurements and made a to-scale diagram of the market area in question. *[handwritten right margin: — can introduce map of grocery store]* Logged into Nita Weapon Registration Department site to ascertain whether the weapons were registered. NWRD's database showed that .22 pistol, serial no. 348X75H498, was registered to Ali Aboud of 61 Hill Avenue, Nita City, Nita, and that .38 caliber Smith & Wesson pistol, serial no. V672952, was registered to Mary N. Burns of 221 Elm Street, *[handwritten right margin: — weapons introduction]* Nita City, Nita. Printed out registrations for both. Checked with NCPD weapons theft database to see if Burns's weapon had been reported stolen and found that the theft of the weapon had been reported by the owner at 9:00 a.m. that morning. Logged into DMV site to ascertain what type of car, if any, was registered to Mary N. Burns at the above address. DMV database showed that a *[handwritten right margin: — same as described by Jones & Aboud]* YR-1, black Chevy Impala was registered to John Burns at the same address, 221 Elm St., Nita City, Nita. Printed out DMV registration for that vehicle. Logged in at law enforcement portal of Nita Department of Public Safety to determine if either Burns had a record and found Mary Burns had none, but John Burns had two convictions for possession of heroin and had been arrested on *[handwritten left margin: criminal history]* numerous occasions on gambling charges in the past five years in Nita City, but that no convictions had resulted. I called the head of the NCPD Vice Squad for further information. Was informed by Lt. Davison that Burns was a suspected numbers runner and more recently a higher up in local organized crime. Davison informed me that if we could get a conviction on Burns that it was likely that he would inform on the leadership in Darrow County organized crime. Pulled Burns's fingerprints from database and compared with latent print previously unidentified on .38 caliber Smith & Wesson pistol taken from Jones. Comparison was positive. Left thumb print on pistol *[handwritten right margin: — very important]* matched left thumb print in Burns's file. Then proceeded to talk to Jones. Informed Jones that I had a lead on the driver of the vehicle that delivered him to the front of Aboud's Market and asked if he would like to cooperate. He asked what was in it for him, so I told him that I'd have to talk it over with the District Attorney. Spoke to the District Attorney on the phone. She informed me that she concurred in Lt. Davison's analysis of the Burns situation and informed me that in return for truthful information from Jones regarding any connection that Burns might have to the Aboud murder, would result in accepting a plea to lesser charges from Jones, presumably accepting a plea to simple robbery and dropping of the murder charges. District Attorney Alifano instructed me to get an arrest warrant for Burns for armed robbery and murder and to execute the warrant as soon as possible. Warrant was obtained on 5/11/YR-0 at 6:00 p.m. from Judge Beckman and was executed *[handwritten right margin: — valid warrant]* immediately. Burns was placed under arrest at 6:30 p.m. at his residence at 221 Elm Street, Nita City, Nita.

6 OFFICER'S NAME	7 OFFICER'S SIGNATURE
Detective Juan Perez	Juan Perez

8 DATE/SUBMITTED MO DAY YR	TIME 24 Hour Clock	9 SUPERVISOR'S NAME	10
5/12/YR-0	300	J. McCormick	Page 3 of 4

NITA CITY POLICE DEPARTMENT
NITA CITY, NITA

ARREST REPORT—CONTINUATION PAGE

1 ARREST NUMBER	2 NAME LAST	FIRST	MIDDLE	3 ALIAS/NICKNAME
3182-YR-0	Jones	Lauren	NMI	Spike

4 COMPLAINANT'S NAME	ADDRESS	PHONE
Ali Aboud	61 Hill Avenue, Nita City, Nita	unknown

5 NARRATIVE

Jones Plea Agreement

5/12/YR-0 Continued investigation in the above matter. Spoke to District Attorney Alifano concerning possible plea bargain for Jones in return for testimony. Ms. Alifano authorized me to tell defendant Jones that in return for truthful testimony regarding Mr. Burns's involvement in the Aboud murder she would dismiss the pending murder charge with leave to reinstate should Jones lie on the stand. She would also dismiss the armed robbery and accept a guilty plea to simple robbery. Following this conversation with Ms. Alifano, I again spoke to the defendant Jones. He again agreed to talk to me, and I communicated Ms. Alifano's offer. He agreed to cooperate only if Alifano put her offer in writing, which I assured Jones would occur. Then took Jones to the courtroom where Burns was about to be arraigned. Burns was sitting in the front row of the courtroom between two plain-clothed officers. There was no one else present in the courtroom. Jones looked in through the window, and I asked him if he recognized anyone; he told me that the man in the middle of the three seated people was Burns and that Burns was the man who had picked him up in the Black Chevy Impala. I then asked Jones if he would give another statement, and he indicated that he would. After Jones gave his statement, based on what he said I checked his cellphone and it showed a call from an unknown caller on 5/9/YR-1 at 10:30 a.m.

robbery around 4pm

Tuesday 3 days after

solid but Jones never asked for these terms

so what? all contracts should be?

6 OFFICER'S NAME	7 OFFICER'S SIGNATURE
Detective Juan Perez	Juan Perez

8 DATE/SUBMITTED			TIME	9 SUPERVISOR'S NAME	10
MO	DAY	YR	24 Hour Clock		
5/12/YR-0			300	J. McCormick	Page 4 of 4

NITA CITY POLICE DEPARTMENT
NITA CITY, NITA

John Burns

ARREST REPORT

1 ARREST NUMBER	2 PRINTS [X]	PHOTOS [X]		3 NAME LAST	FIRST	MIDDLE
3197-YR-0				Burns	John	NMI

4 ALIAS/NICKNAME		5 DATE OF BIRTH		6 AGE	7 SEX	8 RACE/ETHNIC.
N/A		9/4/YR-35		35	M	C

9 ADDRESS	PHONE	10 PLACE OF BIRTH
221 Elm Street, Nita City, Nita	493-4143	Meriden, Nita

11 HEIGHT	12 WEIGHT	13 HAIR	14 EYES	15 COMPLEXION	16 SOC. SEC. NUMBER
5'10"	175	Brown	Hazel	Fair/clear	045-38-6262

17 OPERATOR LICENSE NUMBER & STATE	18 MISCELLANEOUS	19 OCCUPATION
N-3132418		unemployed

20 EMPLOYEE/SCHOOL	21 ADDRESS	PHONE
N/A	N/A	N/A

DETAILS OF ARREST

22 DATE OF ARREST MO DAY YR	23 TIME 24 hr clock	24 HOW ARRESTED
5/11/YR-0	1830	ON VIEW [ ] WARRANT [X] ORDER FOR ARREST [ ]

25 PLACE OF ARREST
221 Elm Street, Nita City, Nita

26 INITIAL CHARGE	27 COUNTS	28 STATUTE	29 OFFENSE JURISDICTION	30 WARRANT DATE MO DAY YR
Murder	1	18-6-102 (1)(b)	Nita City & Darrow County	5/11/YR-0

31 SUBSEQUENT CHARGE	32 COUNTS	33 STATUTE	34 OFFENSE JURISDICTION	35 WARRANT DATE MO DAY YR
Armed robbery	1	18-6-302	Nita City & Darrow County	5/11/YR-0

36 VEHICLE INFORMATION				37 PLACE STORED
LICENSE # N/A STATE N/A MAKE N/A VIN N/A				N/A

38 VEHICLE INVENTORY INFORMATION MO DAY YR
BY N/A

39 COMPLAINANT'S NAME	ADDRESS	PHONE
Ali Aboud	61 Hill Avenue, Nita City, Nita	unknown

CONFINEMENT/BOND INFORMATION

40 DATE CONFINED MO DAY YR	TIME 24 Hour Clock	41 PLACE CONFINED	42 COMMITTING MAGISTRATE
5/11/YR-0	1830	Nita City Jail	Gregory S. Lewis

43 TYPE BOND	44 AMOUNT	45 DATE RELEASED MO DAY YR	TIME 24 HOUR CLOCK	46 RELEASED BY
None	N/A			N/A

DISPOSITION INFORMATION

Monday 2 days after crime

47 DEPOSITION DATE MO DAY YR	48 COURT DOCKET	49 COURT/JUDGE	CITY
	YR-0-CR-324	Darrow County-Superior Court in Nita City	

50 DISPOSITION	51 SENTENCE

52 NARRATIVE	
On 5/11/YR-0, I obtained an arrest warrant for the defendant from Judge Beckman at 6:00 p.m. The warrant was executed by me at 6:30 p.m. on the same date at the home of the defendant Burns at 221 Elm Street, Nita City, Nita. The defendant offered no resistance.	
Also present at the scene of the arrest was the defendant's wife Mary N. Burns. I informed defendant that he was under arrest for the murder of Rachel Carter Aboud on 5/9/YR-0 at 401 Main Street, Nita City, Nita. I informed the defendant of his	RIGHT THUMB

53 ARRESTING OFFICER – NAME AND SIGNATURE	54 DATE/SUBMITTED MO DAY YR	TIME 24 Hour Clock
Detective Juan Perez, NCPD *Detective Juan Perez*		

55 SUPERVISOR SIGNATURE	56 ARRESTEE SIGNATURE
J. McCormick	

NITA CITY POLICE DEPARTMENT
NITA CITY, NITA

ARREST REPORT—CONTINUATION PAGE

1 ARREST NUMBER	2 NAME LAST	FIRST	MIDDLE	3 ALIAS/NICKNAME
3197-YR-0	Burns	John	NMI	N/A

4 COMPLAINANT'S NAME	ADDRESS	PHONE
Ali Aboud	61 Hill Avenue, Nita City, Nita	unknown

5 NARRATIVE

Miranda rights and asked him if he understood them. He said that he did. His wife protested that her husband had been home all day Saturday. I told her she could come down to the police station and make a statement if she wanted to. I took the defendant into custody and brought him down to the station. After he was booked, I asked the defendant Burns if he wanted to talk about it. He responded that he didn't know what I was talking about but that he was more than willing to talk about it because he did not have anything to hide. I informed the defendant Burns of the basic facts of the charges against him. He did not seem to react one way or another. I then again informed him of his rights, and he said that he understood them and would be more than happy to sign a waiver and tell me what he was doing on the afternoon of Saturday, May 9th. He said that he had two alibi witnesses, his wife and a friend, Larry Roberts. Defendant was brought before Magistrate Lewis, who denied bond. Defendant was placed in the lock-up for the night.

[handwritten left margin: Tuesday 3 days after crime]

[handwritten right margin: —Both B.S.]

5/12/YR-0 Investigation continued in the above matter. Defendant was taken out of the lock-up shortly before 9:00 a.m. and taken into the empty District Court courtroom by two plainclothed officers. The three men sat in the front row of the courtroom spectator section. Lauren Jones was brought to the window of the courtroom to ascertain if he could identify the defendant Burns. Jones made a positive identification of Burns as the man with whom he had planned the robbery of Aboud IGA Market. The defendant was then arraigned on murder and armed robbery charges. Later that afternoon, the defendant's wife, Mary N. Burns, and friend, Lawrence Roberts, arrived at the station. They both insisted on making statements that were typed out and sworn to before a notary public.

6 OFFICER'S NAME	7 OFFICER'S SIGNATURE
Detective Juan Perez	Juan Perez

8 DATE/SUBMITTED MO DAY YR	TIME 24 Hour Clock	9 SUPERVISOR'S NAME	10
5/13/YR-0		J. McCormick	Page 2 of 2

STATEMENTS FOR THE PROSECUTION

STATEMENT OF ALI ABOUD*

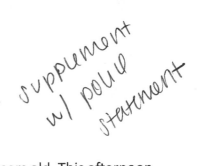
Supplement w/ police statement

My name is Ali Aboud. I live at 61 Hill Avenue, Nita City, Nita. I am forty-six years old. This afternoon, May 9, YR-0, a man tried to rob our store. The name of our store is Aboud's IGA Market, and it's located at 401 Main St., Nita City, Nita. As I said, a man tried to rob our store. He was the same man who was arrested there just a little while ago. He came into the store wearing ordinary street clothes with a blue and white bandana on his face. He had a gun in his hand. He said he wanted all the money out of the register. He got in a hurry and pushed the cash button on my register and reached in and grabbed the bills in the top drawer of the register. I then reached under the counter and grabbed a pistol I had bought for protection and came up real fast and fired a shot. Somehow he had gotten out of the way and the shot hit Rachel. He yelled something about his gun not being loaded. I told him not to move or I'd kill him and ran over to Rachel. She was bleeding really bad. She said, "It was the same car, the same man." She then said some really personal things that I'd rather not say. I believe her first statement meant that the car and the man in the car that was parked outside the store, right in front of the window, facing the wrong way, was the same car she had told me about several times during the past week. She had said that she thought that a man in a black, fairly new American car was planning to rob the store because it kept driving by the store real slow. I didn't think much of it at the time. Maybe if I had listened to her she'd still be alive.

That's all I can remember right now; if you could, please leave me alone.

Name: <u>Ali Aboud</u>
Date: May 9, YR-0

Witness: <u>Detective Juan Perez</u>

Witness: <u>Walter Dolan</u>
Date: May 9, YR-0

---

* This statement was given to Detective Juan Perez at Walter Dolan's house immediately after the robbery.

STATEMENT OF LAUREN JONES*

My name is Lauren Jones. I live at 3800 Hillgrand Drive, Nita City, Nita. I am twenty-eight years old. On May 9, YR-0, I attempted to rob the IGA Market on the corner of Fourth and Main in Nita City, Nita. During the course of that attempt, the owner of the store pulled out a gun from under the cash register counter and tried to shoot me. I ducked, and he shot his wife. Even though I had a gun with me, I did not attempt to fire it. The owner of the store kept me face down on the floor until the police came and arrested me.

I bought the gun from a man who I did not know. The purchase took place the night before in a bar in New City, Nita. On May 9, which was a Saturday, I hitchhiked from New City to Nita City on Route 40, which is a distance of about fifteen miles. It took several rides to reach Nita City. I did not know any of the people who picked me up. The last ride was in a late model black American car. I had the driver leave me off in front of the IGA that I tried to rob. I never intended to hurt anyone; I just needed the money because I am unemployed and I can't get any more money from the State.

I have read this statement that the court reporter transcribed and typed up and it is an accurate transcript of what I said.

NAME: *Lauren Jones*
DATE: May 9, YR-0

SUBSCRIBED AND SWORN TO before me this 9th day of May, YR-0.

Anne Dougherty
Notary Public

* This statement differs from the one he gave on May 12th.
(next page)

---

* This statement was given to Detective Juan Perez at the Nita City Police Station the evening of May 9, YR-0.

STATEMENT OF LAUREN JONES*

My name is Lauren Jones. I live at 3800 Hillgrand Drive, Nita City, Nita. I am twenty-eight years old. I am making this statement because I want to. I have been told what my rights are, and I want to give them up and make this statement. On May 9, YR-0, I was <u>involved in</u> an attempted robbery at the IGA Market on the corner of Fourth and Main. <u>I gave an earlier statement about all this that was not completely true because I was scared</u>. This is the complete truth.

On May 9, I was picked up at the corner of Elm and Fourth by John Burns. I knew John Burns, Burnsey they called him, back from when we were <u>in prison together</u> a lot of years ago. We weren't real close then, but we had run into each other in a bar in Nita City about two weeks before all this happened. We talked some about prison and about how hard it was for ex-cons to find work. I think the name of the bar was McSorley's. Burnsey told me about his plan to hold up a grocery store. He said the guy who owned it was an immigrant type and kept lots of cash round. <u>Burnsey said the only problem</u> <u>was that he had been around casing the place and he was afraid that the owner would recognize</u> <u>him if he pulled it off.</u> He talked me into doing it for him. He said he would drive the job. We talked about when to do it, and he said a Saturday would be best and that he would call me when he was ready. I gave him my phone number. *the car still did not change?*

—10:30am call?

On Saturday May 9, he called on my cell and told me to be on the corner at Fourth and Elm at 3:00 p.m. and to stay there until he got there. When he picked me up, I got into the right front seat. It was sometime between 3:30 and 4:00 p.m. I'm not real sure about the time. Burns started to drive around while we talked. He reached over into the glove compartment, took out a gun and a blue bandana, and handed them to me. I told him that I didn't want a gun. He had said the job was going to be easy because the owner was an Arab guy who was praying all the time. I asked why did I need a gun? He told me that it was just in case. He showed me that the firing pin had been removed and that there were no bullets in it. He said the gun was just to scare the owner.

We pulled by the store once to make sure there were no customers there. <u>Burnsey pulled the car</u> <u>up on the wrong side of the street in front of the store.</u> The car was a pretty new, black Chevy Impala. I put the bandana on before I got out of the car. I went into the store with the gun in my belt. I didn't pull the gun out until I got inside. Everything else happened the way I said in my first statement, except that after the guy shot his wife, I heard Burnsey pull away in a real hurry. That is what happened.

---

* This statement was given to Detective Juan Perez at the Nita City Police Station on May 12, YR-0.

I have read this statement that the court reporter transcribed and typed up and it is an accurate transcript of what I said.

NAME: *Lauren Jones*
DATE: May 12, YR-0

SUBSCRIBED AND SWORN TO before me this 12th day of May, YR-0.

Anne Dougherty
Notary Public

NITA CITY POLICE DEPARTMENT
INTERNAL MEMO*

To: Prosecutor

From: Detective Juan Perez

Re: Follow up

Date: 5/25/YR-1

Using the subpoena obtained by your office, we obtained Lauren Jones's phone records from his cell carrier, National Cellular. He received an incoming call on 5/9/YR-0 at 10:31 a.m. from a prepaid cell that was <u>not a phone number we can establish belonged to John or Mary Burns</u>. I spoke with Jones, who confirmed that that was about when Burns had called him, and I had earlier checked his cell and seen a call at that time. According to the National's records, that cell unit was sold on 1/4/YR-2 with fifty hours of talk time and has never been reloaded. The location from which it was sold, a Quick Mart in Nita City, no longer had any records identifying the purchaser or store videos from the day it was purchased. Both are kept for only one year.

We used the second subpoena your office obtained to get the telephone records for all phones known to relate to John or Mary Burns, and while there were several calls on 5/9/YR-0, we have been able to identify all persons who called them or they called. <u>None were Lauren Jones or anyone connected to him.</u>

We used the final subpoena to impound John Burns's black Chevrolet Impala on 5/14/YR-0. The lab checked it for prints against the exemplar obtained from Jones at the time of his arrest. <u>No prints matching his could be identified.</u> We also had the crime lab process the car for identifiable hairs or fibers. Few were found because the car had been recently washed inside and out and vacuumed. Mrs. Burns told me that her husband had spent a couple of hours doing that on Sunday, 5/10/YR-0, which was Mother's Day, as a present to her. Using exemplars from Lauren Jones's hair and clothing for comparison, <u>none of the few fibers or hairs in the car matched him.</u>

---

* This document was provided in discovery to defense counsel who confirmed with Mr. and Mrs. Burns that the information about the car being washed and vacuumed on Mother's day was correct.

STATE OF NITA	)	IN THE SUPERIOR COURT OF
	)	DARROW COUNTY
	)	STATE OF NITA
v.	)	YR-0 CR 234
	)	
	)	PRELIMINARY HEARING
	)	TRANSCRIPT OF PROCEEDINGS
JOHN BURNS	)	May 19, YR-0

Clerk: Oyez, Oyez, Oyez. Superior Court for Darrow County is now open and in session. All those having cause before this court draw nigh and give their attention according to law. God save the Court and the State of Nita. The Honorable Jayne Perkins presiding. Good morning, your Honor.

Court: Good morning. What's the first case on the docket this morning?

Clerk: Your Honor, we have a preliminary hearing in the case of State v. John Burns.

Court: Very well, is the State ready?

Prosecutor: Yes, your Honor.

Court: What are the charges here?

Prosecutor: Your Honor, the defendant is charged with violations of Nita General Statutes 18-6-302 and 18-6-102(1)(b).

Court: Will the defendant rise? Mr. Burns, you are charged with violations of Nita General Statutes 18-6-302 and 18-6-102(1)(b). How do you plead to these charges?

Def. Att'y: The Defendant pleads not guilty to both charges.

Court: A plea of not guilty on both will be entered. The State may call its first witness.

Prosecutor: The State calls Ali Aboud.

Court: Mr. Aboud, come around. I am told you prefer to swear your oath on the Koran. That is fine. Please raise your right hand. Do you swear that the testimony you are about to give will be the truth, the whole truth, and nothing but the truth?

Aboud: I do, so help me Allah.

Prosecutor: Would you state your name and address for the record, please?

A: Ali Aboud, 61 Hill Avenue, Nita City, Nita.

Q: Are you employed?

A: Yes, I own Aboud's IGA Market on the corner of Main and Fourth in Nita City, Nita.

Q: Where do you pay your property taxes?

A: I pay them at the Darrow County Tax Assessor's Office. Both my home and market are in Nita City and Darrow County.

Q: Are you a United States Citizen?

A: Yes, for thirteen years. I came to this country in YR-20 for my brother's graduation. He got a Masters and PhD from Nita University in Electrical Engineering. I liked it here and was able to get a green card through some family connections. I am from Afghanistan. Even though I have a college degree in accounting from university in Kabul, the degree wasn't any good here, so I worked as a cab driver. After a couple of years I bought the cab with a friend of mine, and we rented a medallion from a company. He drove days, and I drove nights. About ten years ago I started working part time for Mr. Park at the IGA. When he retired in YR-8 I bought the IGA from him.

Q: Were you married to Rachel Carter Aboud?

A: Yes. I met my wife in YR-17. She's an American. We got married in YR-15 after Rachel accepted Islam as a religion and entered the faith. We prayed at the West Nita City Masji.* I had planned to go to Nita City College, but I stayed with the cab while Rachel got her degree in education. We have two children—Ali, who is twelve, and Krista, who is ten. They go to the public school. When they were little, Rachel took care of them and worked as a tutor part-time. When we bought the IGA, Rachel also helped out there. She was very hard working and wonderful. Two years ago she got a full-time teaching job in Nita's Martin Luther King Elementary School. She still came in and helped at the store, especially on weekends. In fact, she had been helping out for a couple of weeks at the store because my employee had been sick.

Q: Directing your attention to Saturday, May 9, YR-0, can you tell us what transpired at about 4:00 p.m.?

A: According to Afghani Muslim tradition we had been closed on Friday. Saturday afternoon had been slow, and Rachel and I were alone in the store. I was cleaning up the counter area, and she was arranging some magazines in the magazine rack that backs up on the front window. We were going to close at 5:00 p.m., so we wanted to tidy up so we'd be ready for business on Sunday, which is usually a busy day for us. Sometime before 5:00, a man came in the store and pointed a gun at me and told me to clean out the cash register. He kept screaming at me to hand over the money or he'd shoot everyone in the store. He then reached around and opened the register and pulled out some money.

Q: How did that make you feel?

A: I was mostly frightened that he would shoot me or, more importantly, Rachel. I was also upset because I had not been to the bank in a few days and had over $1,900 in the cash drawer underneath the tray with the coins and bills. I reached under the counter and pulled out the gun that I had bought for protection and fired one shot real quick. The guy had ducked out of the way. His hand opened, and he dropped the money. The

---

* A masjid [mas gid] is a mosque, a place of worship for those who accept Islam as their faith.

bullet hit Rachel. She screamed and fell to the floor. The robber was on the floor, too, and I pointed the gun at him and told him not to move or I'd kill him. I ran over to Rachel and held her in my arms. There was blood all over the place.

Q: Did she say anything to you?

A: Yes, she said, "It was the same car, the same man." She then said that she always loved me and told me to take care of the children and myself. Then she smiled, closed her eyes, and died in my arms.

Q: What did the words about the car and the man mean to you?

A: Well, we had been held up twice in the past year, once in January and once in April. That's why I bought the gun. I wish I never had. Rachel was real nervous about being robbed again. She had told me on several occasions during the week before she died that a fairly new, black American car had driven by the store real slow. She told me that she thought the driver was planning to rob the store. I didn't think much of it at the time, thinking Rachel was being overly suspicious, but I guess she was right. She must have seen the driver.

Q: What did you do then?

A: Well, I was crying, and I wanted to kill the robber who was still on the floor, but I didn't. As I held Rachel, I used my cellphone and called the police and they got there in a few minutes. I talked to an officer. I was still real upset. They took the robber away.

Q: Looking around the courtroom, can you identify the man who tried to rob your store?

A: Yes, that's him over there.

Q: Your Honor, may the record indicate that the witness has identified Lauren Jones as the man who tried to rob his store on May 9, YR-0?

Court: Any objection?

Def. Att'y: No, your Honor.

Court: The record will so indicate. Mr. Prosecutor, you may proceed.

Prosecutor: Thank you, your Honor. Mr. Aboud, do you remember seeing a black, late-model American car near the time of the robbery?

A: Oh yes, I forgot to tell you. The man who tried to rob the store got out of a pretty new looking, black American car before he came into the store. I noticed it only because the car drove up to the store and parked on the wrong side of the street, right in front of the store. The robber got out of the passenger side and walked around the front of the car into the store. I never saw the car after that. I guess the driver got scared and took off.

Q: Do you remember the license plate number on the car?

A: Not all of it. I'm pretty sure it was a Nita plate with three numbers and three letters, and I remember a K and an 8.

Q: Did you see the driver?

A: Yes, I got a glimpse of his face. He was on the side of the car nearest to me.

Q:	Looking around the courtroom, do you see the driver of the car here today?
A:	Well, I'm not sure, but I think it's that guy over there (pointing).
Prosecutor:	May the record reflect the witness has identified the defendant?
Court:	Any objection?
Def. Att'y:	Not at this time.
Court:	Very well, the record will so reflect.
Q:	Mr. Aboud, had you ever fired your gun before May 9, YR-0?
A:	I bought it only a month before the robbery because the police were never there to protect us when we needed them. Now Rachel is dead. I only fired it the day I got it because I had to take a one-day gun safety course to get my permit.
Prosecutor:	I have no further questions of this witness at this time, your Honor.
Def. Att'y:	I move for production of any statements of this witness in the possession of the State.
Prosecutor:	There is one statement that the State will provide to the defense.
Court:	Any cross-examination?
Def. Att'y:	Yes, just a few questions. Mr. Aboud, I notice that you're wearing glasses. Did you have your glasses on the date of this incident?
A:	Yes, I always do.
Q:	Is your vision corrected to 20/20?
A:	Yes, it is.
Q:	Did your wife wear glasses?
A:	No, she had perfect vision.
Q:	Was she in a position to see the license plate and driver?
A:	Yes, she was right at the window where he drove up.
Q:	Where were the letter and number you think you saw on the license plate?
A:	I don't know.
Q:	How far were you from the driver?
A:	About twenty feet.
Q:	How long did you look at him?
A:	Only a second or two.
Q:	Mr. Aboud, you strike me as an honest man. Isn't it true that you're not sure the defendant is the man who was in the car?
A:	I'm not positive, if that's what you mean. It looks like him, but I'm just not sure.
Q:	Did you give a description of the man to the police?

A: No, they never asked for one, and I was too shaken to think of it.

Q: How far was your wife from the driver?

A: The car couldn't have been more than ten feet away from where she was standing.

Q: Did the magazine rack obstruct her view?

A: No, the rack is only four feet tall, and she was 5′5″ tall.

Q: Were the windows clean?

A: Yes, Rachel washed them every day she was in.

Q: Do you know the defendant?

A: No, I don't.

Def. Att'y: I have no further questions, your Honor.

Prosecutor: Nothing further for the State with this witness, your Honor.

Court: Very well, you may be excused, Mr. Aboud. Does the State have any further witnesses?

Prosecutor: Yes, your Honor, the State calls Lauren Jones.

Court: Come around, Mr. Jones. Do you swear that the testimony that you're about to give will be the truth, the whole truth, and nothing but the truth?

Mr. Jones: I do.

Prosecutor: State your name and address for the record.

A: Lauren Jones, 3800 Hillgrand Drive, Nita City, Nita.

Q: Are you married?

A: No, never.

Q: Are you employed?

A: No, not at this time.

Q: How do you usually occupy yourself?

A: Since the Army, I've worked odd jobs, nothing permanent.

Q: Directing your attention to May 9, YR-0, at about 3:30 p.m., can you tell the court what you were doing?

A: Yes, I was waiting on the corner of Elm and Fourth for John Burns to pick me up.

Q: Were you picked up?

A: Yes, John Burns—he's a guy who had done time at the State Pen while I was there—came by in a YR-1 black Chevy Impala between 3:30 and 4:00.

Q: Why were you waiting for him?

A: Because he called me that morning and told me to be there then. Burnsey and I had run into each other several weeks before in a local bar. We hadn't seen each other since prison. After talking about how good it was to be out, we complained to each other about how rough it was for ex-cons to get jobs. He told me that he really needed some money to help support his family and that he had staked out a grocery store in Nita City that would be easy pickings. Burnsey told me that if I would help him do the job, he'd split the money even. He said the reason he needed help was that he had cased the place too many times and he thought the people who owned it might recognize him if he pulled the job. I was really broke, so I agreed to do it.

Q: What happened after he picked you up?

A: Burnsey drove around for a few minutes. He reached over and pulled a gun and a blue bandana out of his glove compartment. He told me the gun didn't work because the firing pin had been removed, but that I wouldn't have any trouble because the owners would be scared stiff just by seeing the gun.

Q: What did you do then?

A: Well, we cruised by the store once to make sure that there were no customers who might get in the way. I put the bandana on and took the gun. Burnsey pulled over in front of the store, parking on the wrong side of the street right next to the store. I got out of the car, walked around it and into the store.

Q: Who was in the store?

A: Just like he said, there was an Arab guy behind the cash register and a lady wearing that Arab head scarf standing near the magazine rack next to the window. I went up to the guy and told him to give me everything out of the cash register. He didn't move, so I told him that I had a gun. He looked frightened, but he didn't move, so I opened the register and grabbed the money out of the top of the cash drawer. The Arab guy then reached under the counter, and I figured that he was going for a gun. I knew that my gun didn't work, so I dropped the money and hit the deck. I heard one shot fired and the lady scream. I yelled at the guy that my gun wasn't loaded. He told me not to move or he'd kill me, so I stayed put. He went over to the lady and started talking to her. I couldn't hear what they were saying. He called the cops on his cell, and I could hear that he was crying. I guess he killed his wife when he shot. The cops came and arrested me.

Q: What happened to the YR-1 Impala?

A: Right after I heard the shot, I heard some tires screech, so I guess Burnsey just took off, leaving me to fend for myself.

Q: Have you been charged with any offense for your activities on May 9, YR-0?

A: Yes, I pleaded guilty to robbery, yesterday, May 18.

Q: Looking around the courtroom, is the man you referred to as Burnsey present?

A: Yes, that's Burnsey right over there.

Prosecutor: May the record reflect that the witness has identified the defendant, John Burns?

Court: Any objection?

Def. Att'y: No objection, your Honor.

Court:	The record will so reflect. Does the State have anything further?
Prosecutor:	We have no further questions of this witness at this time, your Honor.
Court:	Does the defense have any cross-examination?
Def. Att'y:	Just a few questions, your Honor, but first we would move that the State produce any statements of this witness in its possession.
Prosecutor:	Your Honor, there are two statements that I am providing to defense counsel.

[Whereupon the proceeding paused while defense counsel reviewed the documents.]

Court:	Very well, let's proceed with cross-examination.
Def. Att'y:	Mr. Jones, what is your social security number?
A:	XXX-XX-4748
Q:	Did you spend any time in the military?
A:	Yes, I was in the Army after I graduated from high school here in Nita City. I was discharged in YR-9.
Q:	What type of discharge did you receive?
A:	It was a dishonorable discharge. They trumped up some charges against me, saying that I was stealing crates of cigarettes from the PX, but I was clean.
Q:	Isn't it true, Mr. Jones that you were originally charged with murder as well as armed robbery in this case?
A:	Yes, the murder charge was dropped. Look it, my gun wasn't even loaded. The Arab guy shot his own wife, not me. Lucky for me he didn't know how to use that gun.
Q:	You have entered a guilty plea to simple robbery, isn't that correct?
A:	Yes, I already said that.
Q:	Have you been sentenced on that charge?
A:	No, not yet.
Q:	When will that happen?
A:	I don't know, they haven't told me.
Q:	Will it be after any trial concerning the Aboud robbery and killing?
A:	That's my understanding.
Q:	Are you currently being held in jail?
A:	No, I made bond. My brother put up his house.
Q:	Since you got out of jail, had you ever seen my client before today?
A:	Sure, three times. Once when we met in the bar, once on the day of the robbery, like I said, and then the Tuesday after I got busted. Burnsey was sitting in a courtroom

between two cops in suits. They were the only ones there. I looked in and identified him as the guy who got me in all this trouble, the guy in the black Impala.

Q: Did you tell the police about the man in the black car right after they arrested you?

A: No, it wasn't until after I got arraigned on Monday, May 11, YR-0.

Q: Why did you wait until then?

A: Because when I was in the car with Burnsey, he told me that he was connected, you know, had some tough friends, and said that the holdup was a piece of cake, but that if I screwed up and got caught that I better forget that I ever saw him and that if I said anything about him that it would be a real mistake. I believed him because he had a reputation in the joint as being connected. .

A: When you say "connected," what does that mean?

Q: Being in organized crime.

Q: Mr. Jones, how many times have you been convicted of criminal offenses?

Prosecutor: Your Honor, at this point I'll have to object. Mr. Jones's criminal record is a matter of public record that counsel can easily obtain, and I don't believe that inquiry at this point is necessary or relevant to determining probable cause to hold the defendant for trial.

Court: Objection sustained.

Def. Att'y: I have no further questions, your Honor.

Prosecutor: No redirect, your Honor.

Court: You may be excused, Mr. Jones. Does the State have any further witnesses?

Prosecutor: Just one, your Honor. The State calls Detective Juan Perez.

Court: Detective Perez, do you swear that the testimony that you are about to give will be the truth, the whole truth, and nothing but the truth?

Perez: I do.

Court: Very well, you may proceed.

Prosecutor: Could you state your name and badge number for the record?

A: I'm Detective Juan Perez, Badge No. 914, Nita City PD.

Q: How old are you?

A: Thirty-three.

Q: How long have you been with the Nita City PD?

A: Eleven years.

Q: What did you do before you joined the force?

A: After I graduated from high school in YR-15, I did a four-year hitch in the Navy from which I received an honorable discharge in YR-11. It was right after that that I joined the Nita City PD.

Q:	Have you always been a detective?
A:	No, I started out as a patrolman and worked my way up through the ranks. I became a detective three years ago. That was the same time that I got my BS in Criminal Justice from Nita State University after going part-time for years.
Q:	Have you received any special training while on the force?
A:	Yes, just before I was promoted to detective, I attended the FBI school in Virginia. Since I was scheduled to join the burglary squad, I received special training in fingerprint analysis, including both the techniques of removing prints from suspicious objects and the comparison analysis of those prints with others.
Q:	Directing your attention to May 9, YR-0, did you have occasion to investigate an alleged robbery and murder at Aboud's IGA Market at 401 Main Street, Nita City, Nita?
A:	Yes, I was the chief investigating officer.
Q:	Can you briefly relate what occurred that afternoon?
A:	Yes, may I refer to my reports?
Prosecutor:	With leave of the Court.
Court:	Does the defense have any objection to the detective referring to his reports?
Def. Att'y:	I have no objection as long as we get to see them before cross, your Honor.
Court:	Very well, you may refer to your reports, Detective Perez.
Perez:	Thank you, your Honor.
Court:	You may proceed.
Prosecutor:	Again, Detective, can you briefly state what occurred on the afternoon of May 9, YR-0?
A:	I was called to the Aboud IGA Market at about 4:15 p.m. Upon arrival, I noted that Mr. Aboud was holding a gun on a man later identified as Lauren Jones. Mrs. Aboud was lying in a pool of blood near the magazine rack next to the front window. I checked her, and she appeared to be dead. Mr. Aboud informed me that Jones had tried to rob him and that he, Aboud, had attempted to shoot Jones, had missed, and hit his wife. I put Mr. Jones under arrest and took Mr. Aboud's gun, a .22 caliber pistol, from him and took from Mr. Jones a .38 caliber Smith & Wesson pistol, and put both weapons in individual evidence bags. I was very careful not to smudge any possible prints on either weapon. I took Mr. Aboud to his neighbor's house while other officers took Jones downtown. Mr. Aboud gave me a statement there.
Q:	Did you test the .38 for fingerprints?
A:	Yes, I found a complete set of prints from Jones' right hand and one latent print on the barrel of the weapon just forward of the firing mechanism, with the nail pointing towards the trigger, which I later found to be the left thumbprint of the defendant, John Burns.
Q:	How did you connect Burns with this weapon?
A:	On Monday, May 11, YR-0, I logged into the law enforcement portal at the Nita Weapon Registration Department and saw that the .38 pistol was registered to Mary N.

Burns, the defendant's wife. On the DMV's site, I saw that her husband, Mr. Burns, who lived at the same address, owned a black YR-1 Chevy Impala that was like the vehicle allegedly involved in the robbery. On the State Department of Public Safety Web site I learned that Burns had a record of convictions and arrests including some in Nita City. So, I pulled his fingerprint card and compared it to the previously unidentified print on the .38. The left thumbprint on the card and gun matched perfectly.

was gun reported missing?

Q: What did you do then?

A: I obtained an arrest warrant for John Burns and executed the warrant and took him into custody at 6:30 p.m. that night.

Q: Has anything else of importance happened in regard to this case?

A: Yes, on Tuesday, May 12, YR-0, Mr. Burns was in a show-up where Jones identified him as the man who planned the robbery of the IGA Market on May 9. Also, Mrs. Burns and a friend of Mr. Burns came down to the station on the same day and gave statements.

Prosecutor: I have no further questions of this witness.

Court: Any cross-examination?

Def. Att'y: Your Honor, we would move for production of the reports that the detective used in making his testimony.

Court: Motion is granted.

Def. Att'y: We have no questions of this witness, your Honor.

Court: You may be excused, Detective. Does the State have any more witnesses?

Prosecutor: No, your Honor. At this time we would move that the defendant John Burns be bound over to the Superior Court for trial on the charges of murder in violation of G.S. 18-6-102(1)(b) and armed robbery in violation of G.S. 18-6-302.

Court: The Court finds probable cause on both charges and orders that the defendant John Burns be held for trial without bail on both charges.

DOCUMENTS

NEWS STORY*
May 10, YR-0

Man Misses Robber, Kills Wife

NITA CITY, Nita

Firing at a hold-up man, local grocer Ali Aboud missed his target, and the bullet struck his wife, Rachel, who died in his arms moments later.

The Abouds, co-owners of the IGA Grocery at Fourth and Main, were alone in the store when a masked robber entered. A sobbing Aboud later told reporters, "After the second robbery this year, I went out and bought a gun. When the punk told me to give him all my money, I told him I would. He reached for the money in the cash register, and I reached for my gun under the counter." Aboud, overcome by grief, was unable to conclude his account of the robbery.

Detective Juan Perez of the Nita City Police, the first to arrive at the scene, provided additional details:

"Apparently Aboud had never fired the gun before. The poor guy shot his wife, who was putting magazines on the shelf by the front window."

Perez said police believe Aboud kept the robber pinned down at the same time he rushed to his wife's aid. Police officials have identified the suspect in custody as Lauren Jones of Nita City and have indicated he will be charged with first-degree murder and robbery.

No charges will be filed against Aboud. Rachel Mrs. Aboud spoke to her husband for a few moments before she died. Both Aboud and Detective Perez have declined comment on what she said.

Rachel Carter Aboud was pronounced dead at the scene by Coroner Fred Rothman at 4:28 p.m.

---

* This document was printed on May 10 from www.nitamorningglobe,com/frontpage.story1/05_10_YR-0.

OBITUARY*
May 10, YR-0

RACHEL CARTER ABOUD

Rachel Carter Aboud, 41, a Nita City resident for her entire life, died yesterday from a gunshot wound received during a holdup of the IGA Grocery store she and her husband owned and operated. Mr. Aboud is a native of Kabul, Afghanistan, where he graduated from University and received a degree in Accounting. He emigrated to the U.S. twenty years ago, became a citizen in YR-13, and after owning and operating a cab, became the owner of the IGA store in YR-8.

Mr. and Mrs. Aboud have two children: Ali, age 12, and Krista, age 10. Mrs. Aboud is also survived by her parents, Alex and Stephanie Carter of Nita City, and also her two brothers Robert and Malcolm both of Nita City.

Mrs. Aboud was employed as an elementary school teacher at Martin Luther King Elementary School in Nita City. She was also active in the community, working as an organizer at the Nita City Masjid's soup kitchen.

Funeral services will be held and internment will occur at the Nita City Masjid on May 11, YR-0. In lieu of flowers, the family requests that donations be made to the charitable organization of the donor's choosing.

---

* This document was printed on May 10 from www.nitamorningglobe,com/obituary7/05_10_Y-0.

ESPN ONLINE WORLD SERIES OF BOWLING TV LISTING*
May 9, YR-0

4:00 p.m. ESPN

Pro Bowling HD World Series of Bowling, Las Vegas

$750,000 in prize money and America's best bowlers.

120 mins.

---

* This document was printed from http://espn.go.com/espntv/onair/index/05_09_YR-0/. All listing other than the one appearing above were redacted.

Map of Nita City, Nita

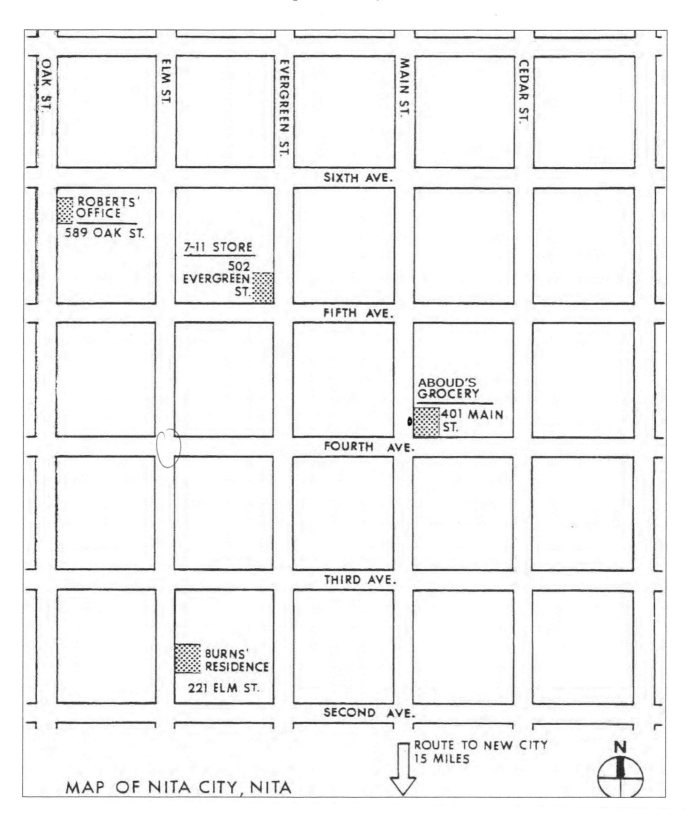

MAP OF NITA CITY, NITA

Diagram of Aboud's Grocery

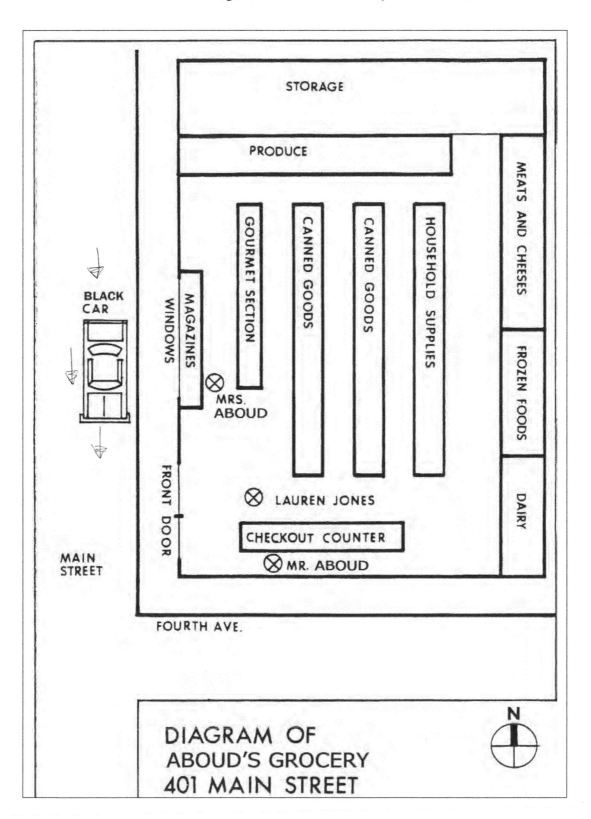

Floor Plan of Burns Residence at 221 Elm Street

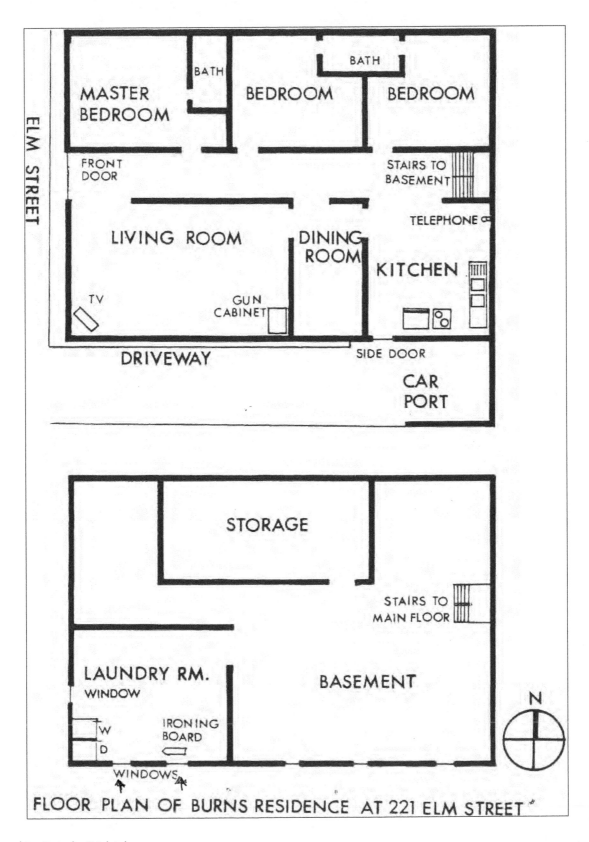

FLOOR PLAN OF BURNS RESIDENCE AT 221 ELM STREET

Uniform Arrest and Disposition Record - Lauren Jones

NAME: Lauren Jones		DOB: 7/31/YR-28	
SS. NO. xxx-xx-4748		POB: Meriden, Nita	
DATE	ADDRESS	OFFENSE	DISPOSITION
2/24/YR-14	707 Williams St. Nita City, Nita	18-6-808 Joyriding	Adj. delinquent Probation 2 yrs.
5/28/YR-13	600 Asylum Avenue Nita City, Nita	18-6-503 Carrying concealed weapon	Prob. violation 1 yr. Training School Released 3/14/YR-12.
9/22/YR-11	735 Clarkson St. Nita City, Nita	18-6-203 Second Degree Burglary	Plea to Misd. Trespass Probation ended 4/10/YR-9.
11/14/YR-9	37 Bainton Road Nita City, Nita	18-6-301 Robbery	5-7 yrs. State Prison Paroled 2/8/YR-5.
4/17/YR-5	925 25th St. Nita City, Nita	18-5-202 First Degree Burglary	5-7 yrs. State Prison. Paroled 8/4/YR-1.
5/9/YR-0	3800 Hillgrand Dr. Nita City, Nita	18-6-102 (1)(b) Murder	Dismissed with leave.
		18-6-302 Armed Robbery	Plea of guilty to Robbery. Sentencing Pending

Alexander McConachie
Alexander McConachie

Superintendent of Documents

Certified as of this 13th day of May, YR-0.

Charlotte Noll
Charlotte Noll

Notary Public

D's record

Uniform Arrest and Disposition Record - John Burns

NAME: John Burns		DOB: 9/4/YR-35	
SS. NO. xxx-xx-6262		POB: Meriden, Nita	
DATE	ADDRESS	OFFENSE	DISPOSITION
2/18/YR-13	2112 York Ave., Apt. 21 Nita City, Nita	18-6-905 Poss. Heroin with Intent to Sell 18-6-906 Poss. Heroin	Dismissed w/o leave Plea Guilty 2–5 yrs. Paroled State Penitentiary 5/12/YR-12
12/3/YR-9	412 N. Salem Nita City, Nita	18-6-906 Poss. Heroin	Plea Guilty 2–5 yrs. Paroled State Penitentiary 11/7/YR-8
4/21/YR-4	221 Elm Street Nita City, Nita	18-6-1104 Gambling	Dismissed with leave
9/14/YR-4	221 Elm Street Nita City, Nita	18-6-1104 Gambling	Dismissed with leave
11/17/YR-4	221 Elm Street Nita City, Nita	18-6-1104 Gambling	Dismissed with leave
3/10/YR-3	221 Elm Street Nita City, Nita	18-6-1104 Gambling	Dismissed with leave
8/7/YR-3	221 Elm Street Nita City, Nita	18-6-1104 Gambling	Dismissed with leave
12/21/YR-2	221 Elm Street Nita City, Nita	18-6-1104 Gambling	Dismissed with leave
5/24/YR-2	221 Elm Street Nita City, Nita	18-6-1104 Gambling	Dismissed with leave
9/18/YR-2	221 Elm Street Nita City, Nita	18-6-1104 Gambling	Dismissed with leave
4/18/YR-1	221 Elm Street Nita City, Nita	18-6-1104 Gambling	Dismissed with leave
12/30/YR-1	221 Elm Street Nita City, Nita	18-6-1104 Gambling	Dismissed with leave

Uniform Arrest Report and Disposition Record - John Burns (Continued)

NAME: John Burns		DOB: 9/4/YR-35	
SS. NO. xxx-xx-6262		POB: Meriden, Nita	
DATE	ADDRESS	OFFENSE	DISPOSITION
5/11/YR-0	221 Elm Street Nita City, Nita	18-6-102 (1)(b) Murder 18-6-302 Armed Robbery	Pending

Alexander McConachie

Alexander McConachie

Superintendent of Documents

Certified as of this 13th day of May, YR-0.

Charlotte Noll

Charlotte Noll

Notary Public

State of Nita Department of Motor Vehicles Registration Record*

			VALIDATION		
	LICENSE NO. **KAM138**				

OWNER'S COPY **Vehicle Reg. Cert.**	VALID TO **Feb. 15, YR+1**		NITA DEPARTMENT OF TRANSPORTATION DIVISION OF MOTOR VEHICLES		
	TITLE NUMBER **17380475**	MAKE **Chev**	STYLE **4 Dr**	YR. **YR-1**	COLOR **BL.**

IMPORTANT: To retain plate, liability insurance must be maintained continuously

VEHICLE IDENTIFICATION NUMBER **E0062EGD14184**		TOTAL FEE **24.00**	
GROSS WEIGHT	CLASSIFICATION	EQUIP. NO.	STATUS

```
MR. JOHN BURNS
221 Elm Street
Nita City, Nita 99993
```

OWNER'S SIGNATURE

John Burns

---

* This document was printed by Detective Perez from a record appearing on the Nita DMV website.

Nita Department of Public Safety Weapons Registration Form - Ali Aboud*

Owner's Name: _____ Ali Aboud _____

Address: _____ 61 Hill Avenue _____

City/State/Zip: _____ Nita City, Nita 99991 _____

Are you a citizen of the United States? _____ Yes _____

Have you ever been convicted of a felony? _____ No _____

Manufacturer of weapons: ___ Colt Arms Co. _____

Model Type: __Pistol _____

Caliber: _____ .22 _____

Serial No.: ___ 348X75H 498 _____

Has the serial number been changed or altered in any way?_ No _____

Date of purchase: ____ 4/12/YR-0 _____

Seller: _The Sport Mart _____

Seller's address: _____ 324 Main Street _____

Seller's city/state/zip: _____ Nita City, Nita 99993 _____

---

* This record was printed by Detective Perez from the Nita Department of Public Safety Weapons Registration website.

Nita Department of Public Safety Weapons Registration Form - Mary N. Burns*

Owner's Name: Mary N. Burns

Address: 221 Elm Street

City/State/Zip: Nita City, Nita 99993

Are you a citizen of the United States?   Yes

Have you ever been convicted of a felony?   No

Manufacturer of weapons: Smith & Wesson

Model Type: Pistol

Caliber: .38

Serial No.:   V 672952

Has the serial number been changed or altered in any way? No

Date of purchase: 8/8/YR-3

Seller: Brown's Pawn Shop

Seller's address: Whitehead Road

Seller's city/state/zip: Nita City, Nita 99992

---

* This record was printed by Detective Perez from the Nita Department of Public Safety Weapons Registration website.

Death Certificate of Rachel Carter Aboud

COPY 1 FOR STATE VITAL RECORDS	REGISTRATION DISTRICT NO. 07　LOCAL NO. YR-0/248	DIVISION OF HEALTH SERVICES · VITAL RECORDS BRANCH MEDICAL EXAMINER'S CERTIFICATE OF DEATH

DECEASED

NAME OF DECEASED				SEX	DATE OF DEATH (MONTH DAY YEAR)	
1. Rachel (FIRST)	Carter (MIDDLE)	Aboud (LAST)		2. F	3. May 9, YR-0	

COLOR OR RACE	STATE OF BIRTH (If not in USA, name country)	COUNTY OF BIRTH	DATE OF BIRTH (Month, Day, Year)	AGE (IN YEARS LAST BIRTHDAY)	IF UNDER 1 YEAR MONTHS / DAYS	IF UNDER 24 HOURS HOURS / MIN
4. White	5a. NITA	5b. Darrow	6. Jan. 23, YR-55	7. 55		

PLACE OF DEATH COUNTY	CITY OR TOWN	NAME OF HOSPITAL OR INSTITUTION IF NOT IN EITHER GIVE STREET AND NUMBER	IF HOSP OR INST (Specify DOA, Emer Rm Inpatient/OP	INSIDE CITY LIMITS (SPECIFY YES OR NO)
8a. Nita	8b. Nita City	8c. Memorial Hospital	8d. DOA	8e. Yes

RESIDENCE—STATE	COUNTY	CITY OR TOWN	STREET AND NUMBER OR RFD NO.	INSIDE CITY LIMITS (Specify Yes or No)
9a. Nita	9b. Darrow	9c. Nita City	9d. 61 Hill Ave.	9e. Yes

CITIZEN OF WHAT COUNTRY?	MARRIED, NEVER MARRIED, WIDOWED, DIVORCED (SPECIFY)	SURVIVING SPOUSE (IF WIFE GIVE MAIDEN NAME)
10. U.S.	11. Married	12. Ali Aboud

SOCIAL SECURITY NUMBER	USUAL OCCUPATION (KIND OF WORK DONE DURING MOST OF WORKING LIFE, EVEN IF RETIRED)	KIND OF BUSINESS OR INDUSTRY	WAS DECEDENT EVER IN US ARMED FORCES? (Specify Yes or No)
13. 024-33-3918	14a. Grocer	14b. Grocery Store	15. No

FATHER'S NAME	MOTHER'S MAIDEN NAME
16. Alexander Carter	17. Stephanie Carletti

INFORMANT'S NAME AND ADDRESS	RELATION TO DECEASED
18a. Ali Aboud, 61 Hill Ave., Nita City, Nita	18b. Husband

CAUSE

PART 1. DEATH CAUSED BY: ENTER ONLY ONE CAUSE PER LINE FOR (A), (B), (C)

CONDITIONS, IF ANY WHICH GAVE RISE TO IMMEDIATE CAUSE (a), STATING THE UNDERLYING CAUSE LAST. 19.		APPROXIMATE INTERVAL BETWEEN ONSET AND DEATH
(a) IMMEDIATE CAUSE	Exsanguination (blood loss)	
(b) DUE TO, OR AS A CONSEQUENCE OF:	Severed aorta	
(c) DUE TO, OR AS A CONSEQUENCE OF:	gunshot wound	5 mins.

PART II. OTHER SIGNIFICANT CONDITIONS CONTRIBUTING TO DEATH BUT NOT RELATED TO CAUSE GIVEN IN PART 1	AUTOPSY (SPECIFY) YES OR NO	ME OR OTHER	IF YES WERE FINDINGS CONSIDERED IN DETERMINING CAUSE OF DEATH
20a. None	20b. Yes	Rothman	20c. Yes

ACCIDENT, SUICIDE, HOMICIDE, UNDETERMINED, NATURAL CAUSES, OR PENDING (SPECIFY)	DESCRIBE HOW INJURY OCCURED (ENTER NATURE OF INJURY IN PART 1 OR PART II)			
21a. Homicide	21b. Struck by bullet fired at armed holdup man			

TIME OF INJURY MONTH / DAY / YEAR / HOUR	INJURY AT WORK (SPECIFY YES OR NO)	PLACE OF INJURY AT HOME, FARM, STREET, FACTORY, OFFICE BLDG, ETC. (SPECIFY)	CITY OR R.F.D.	COUNTY	STATE
21c. May 9 0 4:10 P	21d. Yes	21e. At store	21f. Nita City, Nita, Nita		

CERTIFIER

MEDICAL EXAMINER CERTIFICATION: ON THE BASIS OF THE EXAMINATION OF THE BODY AND/OR THE INVESTIGATION IN MY OPINION, DEATH OCCURRED ON THE DATE AND DUE TO THE CAUSE(S) STATED

DEATH OCCURRED (HOUR)	THE DECEDENT WAS PRONOUNCED DEAD MONTH / DAY / YEAR / HOUR				DATE SIGNED (MONTH DAY YEAR)
22a. 4:15 p. M	22b. May / 9 / 0 / 4:28 p. M				23a. May 10, YR-0

SIGNATURE	ADDRESS	MEDICAL EXAMINER OF (SPECIFY COUNTY)
23b. Brian Blackhouse	23c. County Office Building	23d. Darrow

BURIAL

BURIAL, CREMATION, OTHER (SPECIFY)	DATE	NAME OF CEMETERY OR CREMATORY	LOCATION (CITY TOWN OR COUNTY) (STATE)
24a. Burial	24b. May 13	24c. Nita City Masjid Cemetery	24d. Nita City, Nita

FUNERAL HOME NAME / ADDRESS	SIGNATURE OF FUNERAL DIRECTOR	LICENSE NO.
25. Nita City Masjid, Nita City, Nita	26.	

DATE REC'D BY LOCAL REG.	SIGNATURE OF REGISTRAR	SIGNATURE OF EMBALMER (IF EMBALMED)	LICENSE NO.
27a. 5/13/YR-0	27b. Adrienne Fox	28.	

DHS FORM 2154 REV 1/78

MEDICAL EXAMINER: After you have initiated the Certificate of Death, give copies 1 & 3 to funeral director when body is released, and route copy 2 to Chief Medical Examiner. If cause of death is pending, file Supplemental Report of Cause of Death (Form VS 8A) when the additional information has been obtained. **FUNERAL DIRECTOR:** Copy 1 must be completed and filed with the Local Registrar within 5 days. Copy 3, when signed by the medical examiner is your authorization for final disposition.

IN THE SUPERIOR COURT OF DARROW COUNTY

STATE OF NITA

THE PEOPLE OF THE STATE OF NITA

vs.

LAUREN JONES,
       Defendant.

Case No. YR-0 CR 319

PLEA AGREEMENT

1. I, Lauren Jones, the defendant in this Criminal Action, do hereby withdraw my previous entered pleas of not guilty to ARMED ROBBERY G.S. 18-6-302 and FIRST DEGREE MURDER G.S. 18-6-102(1)(b) and enter plea of GUILTY to a substituted information charging me with ROBBERY G.S 18-6-301, with a maximum sentence of ten years of imprisonment and a $30,000 fine, or both, and a minimum sentence of one year of imprisonment or a $2,000 fine.

2. I understand that if the Court accepts the plea as indicated above, I give up my right to trial by jury, at which I would have the following rights: (a) the right to have a jury determine my guilt or innocence; (b) the right to see and hear witnesses testify and to have my lawyer question them for me; (c) the right to subpoena witnesses in my behalf and present items of evidence in my defense; (d) the right to testify or remain silent; (e) the right to have the prosecution prove my guilt beyond a reasonable doubt, before I can be found guilty.

3. I understand that I give up my right to appeal all matters except the legality of this sentence and the jurisdiction of this Court. I am knowingly waiving all other rights of appeal. My attorney has explained to me what an appeal is and how I can properly file for an appeal should I choose to do so. He has advised me that if I cannot afford an attorney, one will be appointed for me by the Court.

4. I understand that a Plea of Not Guilty denies that I committed the crime; a Plea of Guilty admits that I did commit the crime; and a Plea of No Contest says that I do not contest the evidence against me. I understand that if the Court accepts my plea there will be no trial and the Court will impose sentence based on my plea.

5. I have read the substituted Information in this case, or have had it read to me, and I understand the charge pending against me. My lawyer has explained to me the maximum penalty for the charge, the essential elements of the crime, and possible defenses to the crime, and I understand these things. I understand that if I am on parole, my parole can be revoked and I can be returned to prison to complete that sentence; if I am on probation, my probation can be revoked and I can receive a separate sentence up to the maximum on the probation charge in addition to the sentence imposed in this case.

6. No one has promised me anything to get me to enter this plea, except that the State has agreed to dismiss the Armed Robbery and First Degree Murder charges and to take no position on what sentence is appropriate when I am sentenced for Robbery. I understand that a condition of this plea is that I give truthful and complete testimony at the trial of John Burns and that

should I fail to do so, the State will have the right to reinstitute the ARMED ROBBERY and FIRST DEGREE MURDER charges against me and that my plea of Not Guilty to those charges will be reinstated.

7. I understand my sentence will be imposed within the sentencing guidelines. My presumptive sentence is based on certain factors that have been explained to me. I have truthfully advised the Court about my prior criminal history so that my presumptive sentence can be estimated under the sentencing guidelines. Based on these representations, I understand that my anticipated guideline sentence is one year's imprisonment and no fine.

8. If a background check of my criminal history reveals undisclosed convictions and if these convictions serve to enhance my presumptive sentence beyond that currently envisioned, I will not be allowed to withdraw my plea, but will be sentenced in accordance with the appropriate sentencing guidelines. My lawyer has explained to me the requirement that I be truthful in disclosing my prior criminal history and that my failure to be accurate could result in a sentence that is greater than currently envisioned.

9. I have read every word of this written plea or have had it read to me. I have discussed this plea with my attorney, and I fully understand it. I have been told what evidence the State has to present to a jury, and my attorney has advised me as to what defenses, if any, I may be able to assert in my own behalf. I am fully satisfied with the way my attorney has handled this case. He has effectively assisted me in all aspects of my defense.

10. I have been candid and truthful with my lawyer and have told him everything I know about this case.

11. I understand and agree that if the judge permits me to remain at liberty pending sentencing, I must notify my attorney and bondsman and probation officer of any change of address or telephone number. I also understand that for me to receive the sentence that has been promised by this court, I must honor the following conditions: (a) I must have been truthful regarding my prior criminal history; (b) I must report to the Department of Probation and cooperate with them in the preparation of my pre-sentencing investigation; (c) I must remain at liberty without committing any law violation; and (d) I must return to this courtroom on N/A at to be sentenced by this Court. I understand that the violation of any of these conditions could result in my not being allowed to withdraw my plea and the Court being free to sentence me in accordance with the legal maximums recognized under the law.

12. My education consists of the following: high school.

13. I am not under the influence of any drug, alcohol, or medication at the time I sign this plea. I am not suffering from mental problems that will affect my understanding of this plea.

14. I understand that by entering this plea I am subject to potential deportation if I am not a citizen of the United States of America.

NO ONE HAS THREATENED ME TO MAKE ME ENTER THE PLEA. I AM ENTERING THE PLEA BECAUSE I AM GUILTY. I ENTER THE PLEA VOLUNTARILY OF MY OWN FREE WILL.

SWORN TO AND SIGNED by Lauren Jones in the presence of Defense Counsel on this this 13th day of May, YR-0.

Lauren Jones
_____

CERTIFICATE OF DEFENDANT'S ATTORNEY

I, Brian Brook, Defendant's Counsel of Record, certify that: I have discussed this case with the Defendant, Lauren Jones, including the nature of the charges, essential elements of each, the evidence against him of which I am aware, the possible defenses he has, the maximum penalty of the charges, and his right to appeal. No promises have been made to the Defendant Lauren Jones other than as set forth in this plea or on the record. I believe he fully understands this written plea, the consequences of entering it, and that the Defendant Lauren Jones does so of his own free will. I have reviewed the Discovery in this case and have discussed the evidence in this case with the Defendant Lauren Jones. I believe this plea is in my client's best interest.

Brian Brook
_____
COUNSEL FOR DEFENDANT

CERTIFICATE OF PROSECUTOR

I confirm that paragraph 6 of this agreement correctly states the agreement between the Defendant, Lauren Jones, and the State of Nita.

William Hart
_____
ASSISTANT STATE ATTORNEY

Tangible Exhibits

Smith & Wesson recovered by Detective Perez at Aboud IGA D's gun

Serial number on Smith & Wesson recovered by Detective Perez at Aboud IGA

Bandana recovered by Detective Perez at Aboud IGA

License plate from Burns's Chevrolet Impala

STATEMENTS FOR THE DEFENSE

gun c issue
went missing

STATEMENT OF JOHN BURNS*

My name is John Burns, and I was born on September 4, YR-35, in Meriden, Nita. I have a high school education. I understand that I have a right not to talk and to have a lawyer, but I waived those rights because I haven't done anything wrong, so I want to give this statement and I don't need a lawyer.

I went into the Army a year after high school and was in until I got a medical discharge because I became addicted to heroin because it was readily available where I was. After I got out, I came back to Nita City. I wasn't able to find a job. Desperate for money for drugs, I agreed to transport some heroin from Meriden, Nita, to Nita City. I got pulled over, and when they searched the car they found the heroin. They offered me a deal on the possession with intent to sell charge if I would name the dealer, but when I refused because I was afraid of him, the DA said it was plead guilty to what I was charged with or go to trial, so I pled. I got two to five years. After credit for time served in jail when I didn't make bond and good time credit, I served a little over a year at the Nita State Prison.

I was arrested for possession of heroin in December of YR-9. Because it was a relatively small amount, when I pled guilty I only had to do eleven months.

I went cold turkey in prison and got off smack. I haven't used any since. I married my wife, Mary, eight years ago. We have three kids: John, Jr., six; David, four; and Patsy, three. We live at 221 Elm Street in Nita City. I have drawn a diagram of the house that shows where everything is.

Right after the wedding, I got a job as a bartender at the White Swan Bar. I had that job until about six months ago when the owner sold it and they turned it into another pizza joint. When I was laid off, I was making a little over $600 a week between tips and salary. Right now I'm drawing $235.50 a week in unemployment, and my wife works by taking care of the neighbors' kids while they work. She makes between $80 and $160 each week.

We keep six guns in our house. My family always had guns, so it was not unusual for me to have them displayed at the house. My wife actually owns them because I have a record and can't get a license for them. I removed the firing pins from all of them for the safety of the kids. We keep no ammunition in the house. We have two Remington .22 long barrel rifles, a Winchester 20-20 shot gun, two Mauser pistols I got while in the military, and a Smith and Wesson .38 I bought several years ago from Brown's Pawn Shop.

About a week before I was arrested, I noticed the .38 pistol was missing from the gun cabinet in the living room, which is always unlocked. Neither Mary nor the kids had seen it. I told Mary to report it. For about a week I bugged Mary to call the police. She finally did it this morning. If she had done it when I told her to take care of it, none of this would have happened to me.

We do have some money problems because I'm unemployed. Patsy, our daughter, needs an operation in six months that is considered experimental and is not covered by private or government health

---

* This statement was given to Detective Juan Perez at the Nita City Police Station immediately after John Burns was arrested.

insurance. We don't have the cash to pay for it ourselves. But the house we live in is ours, free and clear. I have to believe we can get a mortgage on it when we need to come up with the money to pay for the operation.

On Saturday, May 9, YR-0, I was home all day except for about an hour and a half in the morning when I went to the Walmart to do the grocery shopping for Mary. I have never shopped or even been in Aboud's IGA. Larry Roberts was coming over in the afternoon to watch the World Series of Bowling Tournament on ESPN. ➡ *Started @ 4*

Larry is a guy I bowl with Tuesday nights in a league. We both belong to the Knights of Columbus, and we met about five years ago at one of their meetings. He's also an insurance agent, and when the kids were born I took out a small life insurance policy through him. As a matter of fact, he has loaned me money to make the last couple of payments on the policy, as I've been short of cash. I've always been honest with him. He knows all about my criminal record.

A little after three, I think it was, Larry called to tell me his work was taking longer than he expected and that he wouldn't be over until about 4:30. I gave him a hard time about working too hard, but told him I would see him then. That's all I remember about the phone conversation. Mary was in the kitchen while I was on the phone with Larry. I remember that she had answered the phone.

After I got off the phone, I went back inside and sat down in front of the television and drank some beer. I was really tired. I had been working around the house all day. I had cleaned out all of the gutters and moved everything around in the attic for Mary.

Mary went downstairs after the phone call. She was doing all the laundry. I could hear the machines while I was watching the Red Sox-Yankees game on television that was on before the bowling. I never left the house between 3:30 and 4:30.

Larry arrived at 4:30. I filled him in on what had happened in the first frames and then we watched the rest of the bowling tournament. I think he left about 6:00.

Sunday was Mother's Day, and the kids and I took Mary her breakfast in bed. We spent the entire day around the house. Monday I went out looking for jobs again, and as I usually do on Mondays, I went to the State Employment Service to get some new leads. They only had two for me. One job was at a bar in Nita City, and the other was a dishwashing job in Meriden. I called right away, but both jobs were taken by the time I got through.

I went home at about 4:30. Just after we sat down to dinner at about 6:30, the doorbell rang. Mary went to answer it. She called for me. I came to the door, and a police officer was standing there. I said, "What is it this time, officer, another gambling bust?" The police have been harassing me for the last five years. I don't know why. They keep arresting me for gambling and letting me go. The officer said, "This time you blew it Burns; the charge is Murder One." I couldn't believe it. Mary started to cry. The officer put handcuffs on me, and they took me downtown. I think the kids were scared to death.

I do remember Lauren Jones from when I was in prison. I was not friendly with him. You are right that the other inmates called me Burnsey. I do know a bar called McSorley's, but don't go there. I have never been there with Jones. I have not seen him since I was in prison. No, I am not connected in any way with organized crime or any gangs, and I certainly was not known for that in prison. I was there for a drug conviction, and I pretty much spent my time getting clean and making myself as invisible as possible.

I have read this statement that the court reporter transcribed, and it is an accurate record of what I said.

NAME: *John Burns*

DATE: May 11, YR-0

SUBSCRIBED AND SWORN TO before me this 11th day of May, YR-0.

Kathy Kennedy

Kathy Kennedy

Notary Public

STATEMENT OF MARY N. BURNS*

1. My name is Mary N. Burns, and I am thirty-three years old. I have been married to John Burns for eight years. We have three children. They are John, Jr., six; David, four; and Patsy, three. We live at 221 Elm Street in Nita City in a house that my father left to us when he died. It is a small house, seven rooms, but we got it free and clear, and not having a mortgage payment is really nice when your husband is out of work.

2. When I married John, he had just gotten out of prison after serving his second term for heroin. He had the drugs because when he came back from the Army he was an addict. He wanted me to marry him just before he was arrested the second time, but I wouldn't do it because I didn't want my babies to be born sick. After he got out of prison the second time, he stayed clean. I've loved him ever since high school, so when he got out of prison and stayed off drugs, I married him. I am sure that he has never used any heroin since.

3. John has been arrested several times since we got married. I think each time it's been for gambling. John doesn't gamble. We never had enough money for him to be able to afford to do that. I don't know why the police keep harassing him. I guess every time a crime is committed, they assume John did it just because he went to jail once before.

4. John is a good provider. Until he lost his job as a bartender at the White Swan, we never had any money problems. He was making about $600 a week. He always handled the finances, and while we never had much money, we always had enough. When he lost his job, everything started to go wrong.

5. Patsy got sick, and now the doctors tell us she needs an expensive operation soon. She has something wrong with her small intestine. The operation is considered experimental, and no insurance will cover it. We do own our house free and clear though and can explore a mortgage for money to pay medical bills if it comes to that, but we have been hopeful that as the operation becomes more common, the insurance that will come with John's next job will pay for it. John goes out every day and tries hard to find work. He's trying so hard, but with so many people out of work and him having a criminal record, it's really hard. Now that this has happened, I don't know if anyone will hire him.

6. I've been trying to help out by taking in some of the neighbors' kids on weekdays. Their mothers have jobs, and they pay me $40 per week for each kid. That comes to $80 to $160 per week. I take care of two to four kids at a time. Usually, I get three kids. John gets about $235 a week from unemployment, but we have no idea how long that will last.

7. John has a gun collection. Some are guns he brought back from when he was in the Army. Some are from his family. He bought a few here in Nita City. The guns are registered in my name because John says there is some law that says that anyone who has been in prison can't own a gun. I think there were six guns; three pistols, two rifles, and a shotgun.

---

* This statement was given to Detective Juan Perez at the Nita City Police Station the morning following John Burns's arrest.

8 The first weekend in May, on Saturday, John and I took the kids to the Nita City Zoo. When we got home, John noticed that one of the guns was missing. He asked me if I knew where the gun was, and I said I hadn't seen it since Thursday when I dusted. The missing gun was a pistol. I don't know enough about guns to know what kind it was. I asked the kids if they had seen the gun, and they said no. John said I should report it missing to the police the first thing on Monday morning. All the next week John kept bugging me to call the police, but I never got around to doing it until yesterday morning.

9 We don't lock the gun cabinet because the guns are only for decoration. John never uses any of them, and all the firing pins had been removed. We don't keep bullets for any of the guns in the house.

10 John usually stays around the house on weekends as after a long week I'm really tired and I need help with the kids. On Saturday, May 9, YR-0, Mrs. Womble, who lives next door, took my kids for the entire day. I take care of her child, Dana, because Mrs. Womble works as a phone installer. That Saturday, Mrs. Womble came over in the morning and said as a Mother's Day present to me, she was going to take my kids for the entire day. I was so thankful.

11 John and I were alone in the house all day. It was so quiet, a beautiful warm sunny day. In the morning, John went to the store and did all the marketing for the week. We always shop at the Acme or one of the big box stores like Walmart. We have never shopped at Aboud's IGA. John's black Chevy was in the carport.

12 That Saturday I straightened up around the house and collected all the kids' dirty laundry. I wanted to make the house look good because John told me that Larry Roberts was coming over in the afternoon to watch bowling on television.

13 Larry called at about 3:30 and asked to speak to John. I was in the kitchen at the time sorting the white and dark loads for the washing machine. I only heard one side of the conversation, but it sounded like Larry told John he was going to come over late.

14 I started downstairs to the laundry room just after John hung up the phone. I told John I would be in the basement for a while doing the wash and ironing his shirts. He said he would yell down if he needed anything. I don't think he ever did that.

15 The laundry room is in the basement. It doesn't have much natural light, only three casement windows just below the ceiling that are the kind that have a well around them in the ground outside. They look out at about ground level on the driveway, which is cement.

16 I stayed in the basement doing the laundry until about 5:00. During the entire time I was downstairs, I did not hear John leave. When I came upstairs, John and Larry were sitting in the living room watching bowling and drinking beer. Larry left just before dinner, which was at 6:30, just like it is every day.

17 During the entire time I was downstairs, I heard the television, even though the washer and dryer were on. I never saw or heard the car pull out of the driveway. I wasn't looking out the window all the time, but I think I would have heard or seen the car pull out if John had gone anywhere.

On Monday, May 11, YR-0, just as I was serving dinner to John and the kids, the doorbell rang. I opened the door, and a man was standing there. He told me his name (I forget what it was) and showed me his police badge. He asked me if my husband was home. When I said he was, he asked if I would get him. John came to the door, and the officer asked him if he was John Burns. The officer handed him a piece of paper and told him he was under arrest for murder. I couldn't believe it. They took him away and he's been in jail ever since.

I have read this statement that the court reporter transcribed from what I said, and it is accurate.

NAME: *Mary Burns*
DATE: May 12, YR-0

SUBSCRIBED AND SWORN TO before me this 12th day of May, YR-0.

Kathy Kennedy
Kathy Kennedy

Notary Public

STATEMENT OF LAURENCE R. ROBERTS*

My name is Laurence R. Roberts. My friends call me Larry. I am thirty-eight years old, and I live at 32 Stony Brook Road in Nita City, Nita. I am a graduate of Nita City Community College in Business. I am married, and I have two children.

I work as a salesman for Mutual of Omaha Insurance Company. I have had the job for about ten years. Before that, I worked as a claims adjustor for Allstate.

I belong to the Knights of Columbus in Nita City. I first met John Burns at one of their functions about five years ago. We became good friends. I know he did some time in jail for using drugs, but that was a long time ago. He's a new man. He would never do anything illegal now. I know he has been arrested several times since then. I don't know why someone in the police department thinks that every time any kind of crime is committed in Nita City, John is the one who did it. He's paid his debt to society and gone straight. If he was still doing anything illegal, I wouldn't have anything to do with him.

John Burns bought a life insurance policy from me four years ago for which he pays monthly. He's the kind of client every insurance salesman wants. Until he was laid off, he always paid his premiums on time. The last few months I've been helping him out by advancing the premiums. I know that the Insurance Salesman's Association says it is unethical to advance premiums to a client, but it's perfectly legal, and I've never done it before. I'm only doing it now because John is a good friend and I trust him completely.

John and I belong to the Tuesday Night Bowling League over at Westbury Lanes. John is an excellent bowler and has about a 190 average. He usually does well enough to keep our team in the running despite my lousy bowling.

On Saturday afternoon, May 9, YR-0, I was supposed to meet John at his house at 4:00 p.m. to watch the World Series of Bowling on ESPN. Earlier that afternoon, I was at my office working because I was four days past the end of the month, and I needed to get my monthly report finished and mailed to the main office. At about 3:15, I realized I would not be able to get my work done and get to John's house by 4:00. I called John's number. Mary answered, and I said hello and asked her to put John on. I told him I was going to be late, and he told me I worked too hard and he was running out of beer. I laughed and told him I would be over by 4:30 and that I would bring some extra beer. He would be there and jokingly added that I shouldn't worry if he wasn't home when he got there. He said if the beer ran out before I got there, he might run out and get a couple of six-packs.

possibly left?

I went back to work. When I looked at my watch again, it was a few minutes before 4:30. I walked out to my car and drove to the 7-Eleven store, which is a block from my office. I picked up two six-packs of beer, got into my car, and drove directly to John's. His house is less than a mile from

---

* This statement was given to Detective Juan Perez at the Nita City Police Station.

the store where I bought the beer. I pulled into his driveway and parked right behind his car, a YR-1 black, Chevrolet Impala, which was in the carport. It was probably 4:40 p.m.

When I got there, John was sitting in his chair watching the television. I was able to catch up on the flow of the tournament from the scorecard in the upper part of the screen. I stayed at his house until after bowling was over at 6:00. While I was in the house, John never left.

I have read over this statement that the court reporter transcribed from what I said, and it is accurate.

NAME: _Laurence Roberts_
DATE: May 12, YR-0

SUBSCRIBED AND SWORN TO before me this 12th day of May, YR-0.

Kathy Kennedy
Kathy Kennedy

Notary Public

Applicable Nita Statutes

Nita Criminal Code—Chapter 40

Section 18-6-101. Definitions

(4) Deadly weapon. A deadly weapon is any thing or instrument which may be used to cause serious bodily injury or death.

Section 18-6-102. Murder in the First Degree

(1) A person commits the crime of murder in the first degree if:

(a) With premeditated intent to cause the death of a person other than himself, he causes the death of that person or of another person; or

(b) Acting either alone or with one or more persons, he commits or attempts to commit arson, robbery or armed robbery, burglary, kidnapping, rape, or any sexual offense prohibited by sections 18-3-402 through 18-3-404, and in the course of or in furtherance of the crime that he is committing or attempting to commit, or the immediate flight therefrom, the death of a person, other than one of the participants, is caused.

(2) Murder in the first degree is a class 1 felony.

Section 18-6-301. Robbery

(1) A person or one with whom he participates who takes anything of value from the person or presence of another by the use of force, threats, or intimidation commits robbery.

(2) Robbery is a class 4 felony.

Section 18-6-302. Armed Robbery

(1) A person who uses a deadly weapon in committing a robbery commits armed robbery.

(2) Armed robbery is a class 3 felony.

Section 18-6-401. Felonies Classified Penalties

Felonies are divided into five classes, which are distinguished from one another by the following ranges of authorized penalties upon conviction:

Class	Minimum Sentence	Maximum Sentence
1	Life imprisonment	Life imprisonment
2	Ten years imprisonment	Fifty years imprisonment
3	Five years imprisonment	Forty years imprisonment
4	One year imprisonment, or two thousand dollars fine	Ten years imprisonment, thirty thousand dollars fine, or both
5	One year imprisonment, or one thousand dollars fine	Five years imprisonment, fifteen thousand dollars fine, or both

Applicable Nita Case Law

Rulings of the Nita Supreme Court

1. In the State of Nita, the Supreme Court has held that a gun unloaded or incapable of firing is per se a deadly weapon.

2. The Nita Supreme Court recently considered the question of whether a participant in the commission of one of the felonies enumerated in 18-6-102(1)(b) can be convicted of felony murder where one nonparticipant is killed by another nonparticipant resisting the felony. It ruled that a conviction under those circumstances is within the intent of the statute as long as the killing is the proximate result of actions on the part of one or more of the participants of the criminal conduct that was provocative of lethal resistance by a nonparticipant who in fact killed another nonparticipant as a result thereof. In making that holding, the Nita Supreme Court stated that the mere brandishing of a deadly weapon by a participant in an enumerated crime is not "per se" an "act provocative of lethal resistance." The brandishing of a deadly weapon by a participant must be considered in light of all of the surrounding circumstances to determine if it is one "provocative of lethal resistance."

unloaded gun still deadly

NITA GENERAL JURY INSTRUCTIONS

I. PRELIMINARY INSTRUCTIONS GIVEN PRIOR TO EVIDENCE IF REQUESTED

Nita Instruction 01:01—Introduction

You have been selected as jurors and have taken an oath as jurors. You will be responsible for determining what are or are not the facts of this case based on the law as I explain it to you.

When we take recesses, you may not talk about this case among yourselves or with anyone else. This bar against talking about this case with anyone includes any discussions over the Internet, by e-mail or text, or through social media of any kind.

Until after you have completed your jury service and been discharged from your oath by the Court, do not talk to any of the parties, their lawyers, or any of the witnesses.

If any attempt is made by anyone to talk to you concerning the matters here under consideration in person, in writing, by telephone, or in any other manner, you must report that to me immediately.

Keep an open mind. Do not reach a conclusion or form or express an opinion about the case until you have heard all of the evidence, the arguments of counsel, and my final instructions.

Nita Instruction 01:02—Conduct of the Trial

First, the attorneys will have an opportunity to make opening statements. These statements are not evidence and should be considered only as a preview of what the attorneys expect the evidence will be.

Following the opening statements, witnesses will be called to testify. They will be placed under oath and questioned by the attorneys. Documents and other tangible exhibits may also be received as evidence. If an exhibit is given to you to examine, you should examine it carefully, individually, and without any comment.

It is counsel's right and duty to object when testimony or other evidence is being offered that he or she believes is not admissible. When I sustain an objection to a question, disregard the question. When I sustain an objection to any evidence or tell you to ignore it, you must disregard that that evidence and if a question was asked, the question as well. When I overrule an objection to any evidence, do not give that evidence any more weight than if the objection had not been made.

When the evidence is completed, the attorneys will make final arguments. These final arguments are not evidence, but are given to help you evaluate the evidence. The attorneys are also permitted to argue in an attempt to persuade you to a particular verdict. You may accept or reject those arguments as you see fit.

Finally, just before you go to the jury room to consider your verdict, I will give you further instructions on the law that applies to this case.

II. FINAL INSTRUCTIONS

Nita Instruction 1:01—Introduction

Members of the jury, the evidence and arguments in this case have been completed, and I will now instruct you as to the law. Your verdict must be unanimous—that is, each of you must agree with the verdict.

I will begin with the law applicable to all criminal cases and end with the law applicable to this specific criminal case.

The law you are to apply is stated in these instructions, and it is your duty to follow all of these instructions. You must not single out certain instructions and disregard others.

It is your duty to determine the facts and to determine them only from the evidence in this case. You are to apply the law to the facts and in this way decide the case. You must not be governed or influenced by sympathy or prejudice for or against any party in this case.

Your verdict must be based on evidence and not on speculation, guess, or conjecture.

Do not concern yourselves with the reasons for my rulings on the admissibility of evidence. You must disregard questions, answers, and exhibits that were withdrawn or to which objections were sustained. You should also disregard testimony and exhibits that the Court has refused or told you to disregard. Do not consider any evidence that was received for a limited purpose for any other purpose. The evidence that you should consider consists only of the testimony of the witnesses and the exhibits the court has received.

You should consider all the evidence in the light of your own observations and experiences in life.

Nita Instruction 1:02—Opening Statements and Closing Arguments

Opening statements are made by the attorneys to acquaint you with the facts they expect to prove. Closing arguments are made by the attorneys to discuss the facts and circumstances in the case and should be confined to the evidence and to reasonable inferences to be drawn therefrom. Neither opening statements nor closing arguments are evidence, and any statement or argument made by the attorneys that is not based on the evidence should be disregarded.

Nita Instruction 1:03—Credibility of Witnesses

You are the sole judges of the credibility of the witnesses and of the weight to be given to the testimony of each witness. In determining what credit is to be given any witness, you may take into account his or her ability and opportunity to observe; his or her manner and appearance while testifying; any interest, bias, or prejudice he or she may have; the reasonableness of his or her testimony considered in the light of all the evidence; and any other factors that bear on the believability and weight of the witness's testimony.

Nita Instruction 3:01—Indictment

The indictment in this case is the formal method of accusing the defendant of a crime and placing him on trial. It is not any evidence against the defendant and does not create any inference of guilt.

Nita Instruction 3:02—Burden of Proof

The State has the burden of proving every essential element of any crime charged. The State must prove each element beyond a reasonable doubt. This burden remains on the State throughout the case. The defendant is not required to prove his innocence.

Nita Instruction 3:03—Reasonable Doubt

Reasonable doubt means a doubt based on reason and common sense that arises from a fair and rational consideration of all the evidence or lack of evidence in the case. It is a doubt that is not vague, speculative, or imaginary. It is a doubt as would cause reasonable persons to hesitate to act in matters of importance to themselves.

Nita Instruction 3:04—Presumption of Innocence

The defendant is presumed to be innocent of the charges against him. This presumption remains with him throughout every stage of the trial and during your deliberations on the verdict. The presumption is not overcome until, from all the evidence in the case, you are convinced beyond a reasonable doubt that the defendant is guilty.

Nita Instruction 3:05—Reputation/Character

The defendant has introduced evidence of his character and reputation for [insert trait(s)]. This evidence may be sufficient when considered with the other evidence in the case to raise a reasonable doubt of the defendant's guilt. However, if from all the evidence in the case you are satisfied beyond a reasonable doubt of the defendant's guilt, then it is your duty to find him guilty, even though he may have a good reputation for [insert trait(s)].

Instructions Specific to this Case

The State of Nita has charged the defendant, John Burns, with the crimes of Armed Robbery and First Degree Murder.

Armed Robbery

Under the criminal code of the State of Nita, a person commits the crime of Armed Robbery if he, or one with whom he participates, takes anything of value from the person or presence of another by the use of force, threats or intimidation, and a deadly weapon.

To sustain the charge of Armed Robbery, the State must prove the following four propositions:

(1) That defendant, or one with whom he participated, took something;

(2) That the thing taken was of value;

(3) That the thing taken was from the person or presence of another; and

(4) That the thing was taken by the use of force, threats or intimidation, and a deadly weapon.

I instruct you that under the law of the State of Nita a real gun, whether capable of firing or not, is a deadly weapon.

If you find from your consideration of all the evidence that each of these four propositions has been proved beyond a reasonable doubt, then you should find the defendant guilty of Armed Robbery.

If, on the other hand, you find from your consideration of all the evidence that any one of these four propositions has not been proved beyond a reasonable doubt, then you should find the defendant not guilty of Armed Robbery.

Murder

Under the criminal code of the State of Nita, a person commits the crime of First Degree Murder if acting either alone or with one or more persons, he commits or attempts to commit the crime of Armed Robbery; and in the course of or in furtherance of the crime, or the immediate flight therefrom, the death of a person, other than one of the participants, is caused.

To sustain the charge of First Degree Murder, the State must prove the following two propositions:

(1) That defendant acting with one or more persons committed, or attempted to commit, the crime of Armed Robbery; and

(2) That in the course of or in the furtherance of that Armed Robbery, or the immediate flight therefrom, the death of Rachel Carter Aboud resulted from Mr. Aboud shooting and killing his wife in response to an act of the Defendant, acting with Lauren Jones, in committing an act provocative of lethal resistance.

If you find from your consideration of all the evidence that each of these two propositions has been proved beyond a reasonable doubt, then you should find the defendant guilty of First Degree Murder.

If, on the other hand, you find from your consideration of all the evidence that any one of these two propositions has not been proved beyond a reasonable doubt, then you should find the defendant not guilty of First Degree Murder.

Proximate Cause

The death of Rachel Aboud must have been proximately caused by the conduct of defendant or someone acting in concert or in partnership with defendant. Proximate cause means that cause which in its natural and probable sequence produced the death of the victim, Rachel Aboud. It is the cause without which the death would not have occurred.

If you find that the death of Rachel Aboud was not proximately caused by the defendant's conduct, or the conduct of a person acting in concert or in partnership with the defendant, or if you have a reasonable doubt with respect thereto, then your verdict must be not guilty.

Nita Instruction 1:06–Concluding Instruction

I have no opinion about what has or has not been proven in the case, or as to what are or are not the facts of the case. Those are questions you must answer.

All of my instructions must be taken, read, and considered together as they are connected with and related to each other as a whole.

Do not consider the wisdom of any rule of law. Regardless of any opinions you have as to what the law ought to be, it is your sworn duty to base your verdict on the law I have given you in my instructions.

When you retire to deliberate, elect one of your number to be your foreperson and to guide you in your deliberations. The foreperson will be the person who, if you reach a unanimous verdict, will sign that verdict for the jury. [Judge to explain verdict form.]

A final note: if during your deliberations you have questions about what the evidence has or has not been, you must rely on your collective memory of the testimony. On the other hand, if you have questions about what the law is, I may be able to answer those for you. If legal questions arise, ask the jury attendant to let me know, and I will bring you back into the courtroom to deal with your questions.

NITA covers the key areas of trial advocacy.

Skills-based focus gives you the insight and experience necessary to take your advocacy to the next level.

Our publications are designed to help lawyers develop and refine their advocacy skills in every stage of litigation. Whether it's written discovery, e-discovery, deposition, trial preparation, appeals, or alternative dispute resolution, our books give you the tools to do it all with confidence.

If you're looking for practical skills advice, we have books ranging from how to handle an administrative agency case to preparing trial notebooks to winning appeals.

Visit our online bookstore for the complete NITA collection.

Modern Trial Advocacy

The Effective Deposition

Problems in Trial Advocacy

Statutory Interpretation

Effective Courtroom Advocacy

Federal Rules of Evidence with Objections

Winning on Appeal:
Better Briefs & Oral Argument

Winning At Trial

DON'T DELAY—ORDER TODAY!

GO TO www.lexisnexis.com/NITA
CALL toll-free 800.533.1637